Industrial Policy and International Trade

CONTEMPORARY STUDIES IN ECONOMIC AND FINANCIAL ANALYSIS, VOLUME 62

Editors: Professor Edward I. Altman and Ingo Walter, Associate Dean,
Graduate School of Business Administration,
New York University

Contemporary Studies in Economic and Financial Analysis

An International Series of Monographs

Edited by **Robert J. Thornton** and **J. Richard Aronson**

Volume 1 - *Hunt, L.* - **Dynamics of Forecasting Financial Cycles**

Volume 2 - *Dreyer, J.S.* - **Composite Reserve Assets in the International Money System**

Volume 3 - *Altman, E.I., et al.* - **Application of Classification Techniques in Business, Banking and Finance**

Volume 4 - *Sinkey, J.F.* - **Problems and Failed Institutions in the Commercial Banking Industry**

Volume 5 - *Ahlers, D.M.* - **A New Look at Portfolio Management**

Volume 6 - *Sciberras, E.* - **Multinational Electronic Companies and National Economic Policies**

Volume 7 - *Allen, L.* - **Venezuelan Economic Developement: A Politico-Economic Analysis**

Volume 8 - *Gladwin, T.N.* - **Environment Planning and the Multinational Corporation**

Volume 9 - *Kobrin, S.J.* - **Foreign Direct Investment, Industrialization and Social Change**

Volume 10 - *Oldfield, G.S.* - **Implications of Regulation on Bank Expansion: A Simulation Analysis**

Volume 11 - *Ahmad, J.* - **Import Substitution, Trade and Development**

Volume 12 - *Fewings, D.R.* - **Corporate Growth and Common Stock Risk**

Volume 13 - *Stapleton, R.C. and M.G. Subrahmanyam* - **Capital Market Equillibrium and Corporate Financial Decisions**

Volume 14 - *Bloch, E. and R.A. Schwartz* - **Impending Changes for Securities Markets: What Role for the Exchange**

Volume 15 - *Walker, W.B.* - **Industrial Innovation and International Trading Performance**

Volume 16 - *Thompson, J.K.* - **Financial Policy, Inflation and Economic Development: The Mexican Experience**

Volume 17 - *Omitted from Numbering*

Volume 18 - *Hallwood, P.* - **Stabilizationof International Commodity Markets**

Volume 19 - *Omitted from Numbering*

Volume 20 - *Parry, T.G.* - **The Multinational Enterprise: International Investment and Host-Country Impacts**

Volume 21 - *Roxburgh, N.* - **Policy Responses to Resource Depletion: The Case of Mercury**

Volume 22 - *Levich, R.M.* - **The International Money Market: An Assessment of Forecasting Techniques and Market Efficiency**

Volume 23 - *Newfarmer, R.* - **Transnational Conglomerates and the Economics of Dependent Development**

Volume 24 - *Siebert, H. and A.B. Anatal* - **The Political Economy of Environmental Protection**

Volume 25 - *Ramsey, J.B.* - **Bidding and Oil Leases**

Volume 26 - *Ramsey, J.B.* - **The Economics of Exploration for Energy Resources**

Volume 27 - *Ghatak, S.* - **Technology Transfer to Developing Countries: The Case of the Fertilizer Industry**

Volume 28 - *Pastre, O.* - **Multinationals: Bank and Corporation Relationships**

Volume 29 - *Bierwag, G.O.* - **The Primary Market for Municipal Debt: Bidding Rules and Cost of Long Term Borrowing**

Volume 30 - *Kaufman, G.G.* - **Efficiency in the Municipal Bond Market: The Use of Tax Exempt Financing for "Private" Purposes**

Volume 31 - *West, P.* - **Foreign Investment and Technology Transfer: The Tire Industry in Latin America**

Volume 32 - *Uri, N.D.* - **Dimensions of Energy Economics**

Volume 33 - *Balabkins, N.* - **Indigenization and Economic Development: The Nigerian Experience**

Volume 34 - *Oh, J.S.* - **International Financial Management: Problem, Issues and Experience**

Volume 35 - *Officer, L.H.* - **Purchasing Power Parity and Exchange Rates: Theory Evidence and Relevance**

Volume 36 - *Horwitz, B. and R. Kolodny* - **Financial Reporting Rules and Corporate Decisions: A Study of Public Policy**

Volume 37 - *Thorelli, H.B. and G.D. Sentell* - **Consumer Emancipation and Economic Development**

Volume 38 - *Wood, W.C.* - **Insuring Nuclear Power: Liability, Safety and Economic Efficiency**

Volume 39 - *Uri, N.D.* - **New Dimensions in Public Utility Pricing**

Volume 40 - *Cross, S.M.* - **Economic Decisions Under Inflation: The Impact of Accounting Measurement Error**

Volume 41 - *Kaufman, G.G.* - **Innovations in Bond Portfolio Management: Immunization and Duration Analysis**

Volume 42 - *Horvitz, P.M. and R.R. Pettit* - **Small Business Finance**

Volume 43 - *Plaut, S.E.* - **Import Dependence and Economic Vulnerability**

Volume 44 - *Finn, F.J.* - **Evaluation of the Internal Processes of Managed Funds**

Volume 45 - *Moffitt, L.C.* - **Strategic Management: Public Planning at the Local Level**

Volume 46 - *Thornton, R.J., et al.* - **Reindustrialization: Implications for U.S. Industrial Policy**

Volume 47 - *Askari, H.* - **Saudi Arabia's Economy: Oil and the Search for Economic Technology Transfer in Export Processing Zones**

Volume 48 - *Von Pfeil, E.* - **German Direct Investment in the United States**

Volume 49 - *Dresch, S.* - **Occupational Earnings, 1967-1981: Return to Occupational Choice, Schooling and Physician Specialization**

Volume 50 - *Siebert, H.* - **Economics of the Resource-Exporting Country Intertemporal Theory of Supply and Trade**

Volume 51 - *Walton, G.M.* - **The National Economic Policies of Chile**

Volume 52 - *Stanley, G.* - **Managing External Issues: Theory and Practice**

Volume 53 - *Nafziger, E.W.* - **Essays in Entrepreneurship, Equity and Economic Development**

Volume 54 - *Lea, M. and K.E. Villani* - **Tax Policy and Housing**

Volume 55 - *Slottje, D. and J. Haslag* - **Macroeconomic Activity and Income Inequality in the United States**

Volume 56 - *Thornton, R.F. and J.R. Arnson* - **Forging New Relationships Among Business, Labor and Government**

Volume 57 - *Putterman, L.* - **Peasants, Collectives and Choice: Economic Theory and Tanzania's Villages**

Volume 58 - *Baer, W. and J.F. Due* - **Brazil and the Ivory Coast: The Impact of International Lending, Investment and Aid**

Volume 59 - *Emanuel, H., et al.* - **Disability Benefits: Factors Determining Applications and Awards**

Volume 60 - *Rose, A.* - **Forecasting Natural Gas Demand in a Changing World**

Volume 61 - *Marton, K.* - **Multinationals, Technology and Industrialization: A Study of the Implications and Impact in Third World Countries**

Volume 62 - *Canto, V.A. and J.K. Dietrich* - **Industrial Policy and Industrial Trade**

Volume 63 - *Kimura, Y.* - **The Japaneese Semiconductor Industry**

Volume 64 - *Thornton, R., Hyclak, T. and J.R. Aronson* - **Canada at the Crossroads: Essays on Canadian Political Economy**

Volume 65 - *Hausker, A.J.* - **Fundamentals of Public Credit Analysis**

Volume 66 - *Looney, R.* - **Economic Development in Saudi Arabia: Consequences of the Oil Price Decline**

Volume 67 - *Askari, H.* - **Saudi Arabia's Economy: Oil and the Search for Economic Development**

Volume 68 - *Godfrey, R.* - **Risk Based Capital Charges for Municipal Bonds**

Industrial Policy and International Trade

Edited by VICTOR A. CANTO
Laffer and Canto Associates

J. KIMBALL DIETRICH
University of Southern California
Los Angeles

JAI PRESS INC.

Greenwich, Connecticut *London, England*

Library of Congress Cataloging-in-Publication Data

Industrial policy and international trade
(Contemporary studies in economic and financial analysis ; v. 62)
Includes bibliographic references.
1. United States—Commercial policy—Congresses. 2. Industry and state—United States—Congresses. 3. International trade—Congresses. 4. United States—Economic policy—1981—Congresses. 5. United States—Manufactures—Government policy—Congresses. 6. United States—Foreign economic relations—Congresses. 7. International economic relations—Congresses. 8. Technology transfer—Econmic aspects—Congresses. 9. Free trade—United States—Congresses. 10. Protectionism—United States—Congresses. 11. Competition, International—Congresses. I. Canto, Victor A. II. Dietrich, J. Kimball. III. Series.
HF1455.I488 1992
382'.3'0973—dc20 92-6374
ISBN 0-89232-840-1

55 Old Post Road, No. 2
Greenwich, Connecticut 06836

JAI PRESS LTD.
118 Pentonville Road
London N1 9JN
England

ISBN: 0-89232-840-1

Library of Congress Catalog Card Number: 92-6374

Manufactured in the United States of America

CONTENTS

LIST OF CONTRIBUTORS

Tamir Agmon	Schools of Business University of Southern California Los Angeles
William A. Brock	Department of Economics University of Wisconsin Madison
Tim S. Campbell	Schools of Business University of Southern California Los Angeles
Victor A. Canto	President Laffer and Canto Associates
Truman A. Clark	Vice President Wells Fargo Nikko Investment Advisors
J. Kimball Dietrich	Schools of Business University of Southern California Los Angeles
Sebastian Edwards	Anderson Graduate School of Management Los Angeles
Arthur B. Laffer	Laffer and Canto Associates
Stephen P. Magee	Department of Finance University of Texas at Austin

Gerald Nickelsburg — Marketing Department
McDonnell Douglass Aircraft Company

Lee Price — Joint Economic Committee
U.S. Congress

Gary R. Saxonhouse — Department of Economics
University of Michigan
Ann Arbor

Edward Tower — Department of Economics
Duke University
Durham

Leslie Young — Department of Finance
University of Texas at Austin

ACKNOWLEDGMENTS

The papers and comments which make up *Industrial Policy and International Trade* were presented at a conference sponsored by the School of Business at the University of Southern California in the spring of 1984. The conference was organized by the editors of the volume, both then professors at the university. While much has changed on the international trade scene since the conference, much has stayed the same. At the time of the conference, the U.S. dollar was close to its historic high. Major goverenment interventions such as the Plaza Accord in 1985 to reduce the dollar exchange rate and the semiconductor computer chip agreement between the United States and Japan, and many other international trade interventions, lay ahead. In this election year in the United States, restrictive trade policies are discussed in the light of record Japanese trade surpluses with the United States and many presidential candidates are issuing renewed calls for industrial policy. While many of the particulars of the policy environment and the policy proposals debated today are different from 1984, the basic arguments and political issues represented by participants in the current debate are surprisingly unchanged from those presented by the participants in the USC conference eight years ago. The contributions in this book are only slightly revised since 1984, yet they continue to be relevant to the policy debate concerning industrial policy and international trade, providing insights into the positions adopted by current academics, politicians, businessmen, and workers' representatives.

INTRODUCTION

Victor A. Canto and J. Kimball Dietrich

Following World War II, the United States led the world in advocating free trade policies and supported the establishment of international organizations, such as the International Monetary Fund (IMF), the General Agreement on Tariffs and Trade (GATT), and the United Nations, to promote free trade and the integration of the world economy. These policies produced epic growth in the economies of the world, accompanied by record levels of international trade and economic interdependence among free economies without parallel in history. However, over the last decade there has been an accelerating retreat in the United States from the commitment to the free trade policies responsible for the unique record of postwar economic growth.

In the United States, wages for some industrial goods have increased out of line with average compensation in the manufacturing sector and productivity through union bargaining pressure, as in the case of steel. At the other extreme, some wages were held artificially high by minimum wages, as in the case of textiles. In both cases it appears that labor costs are out of line with market conditions. Additional cost pressures came in the wake of environmentalism and required investments in pollution control, not to speak of numerous regulatory interventions in the form of safety and health requirements. These factors, in addition to reducing incentives to replace older plants and obsolete technology, also reduced the cost advantage of domestic products.

Producers and consumers seeking relatively cheap sources of basic industrial products have followed the path of least resistance. As a result, a reallocation of world patterns of trade has been effected by relocating in countries with lower labor costs, less burdensome regulation, and favorable tax climates. New investments there could also be state of the art technologically, further increasing foreign suppliers' cost advantages. In addition to competition from traditional large industrial powers, newly industrialized nations such as Brazil, Hong Kong, and Korea have penetrated the markets of the United States and Europe. These newly emerging competitors have produced slower growth and even decline in many established sectors of the U.S. economy. This is not a surprising result; historically, international trade has been the means whereby differences in relative prices were arbitraged away by users of traded goods, increasing demand in low-cost supplying countries and reducing orders from U.S. suppliers.

The unfettered market responds by unleashing forces to remove cost imbalances internationally. Wage adjustments are made in uncontrolled markets as workers accept lower pay rather than lose their jobs. Pay reductions in real terms can occur as inflation lowers purchasing power of wages which do not increase to offset higher prices. Productivity increases can occur through greater flexibility in work rules. Reductions in production to cost competitive levels can occur with layoffs and plant shutdowns. Production can shift to the highest marginal products. New investment can take advantage of labor saving technology and energy efficient processes.

Many factors can prevent these economic adjustments from restoring the international equality of relative prices. Unions may negotiate cost of living adjustments (COLAs) in wage agreements preventing real labor costs from falling with inflation, or minimum wages, as mentioned above, may prevent downward adjustments necessary to achieve worldwide balance. Firms operating in these conditions because of union agreements, government regulations, or other rigidities, may choose production or quantity rather than price adjustments to achieve profitability or reduce losses, producing persistent unemployment in affected industries.

Advocates offer "industrial policy" as an alternative to free market adjustments resulting from the changes in relative costs across countries (i.e., further government interventions) to reduce cost differentials through taxes and subsidies or to reduce competition from abroad through trade restrictions. The costs to vocal unions and capital investors during the adjustment can be high, and government representatives can easily be induced to endorse the view that government guided adjustment is better and fairer than adjustment due to unregulated market forces.

The important questions are whether these government guided adjustments are indeed less costly than those resulting from market forces, whether these policies can really be only temporary rather than permanent protections to affected industries, and whether in fact the policies are effective in producing the desired results of lowered adjustment costs. Another question is: Does regulation breed further regulation?

Since real wages and returns to capital with government assistance do not adjust to restore comparative advantage, income levels may be maintained at the expense of the taxpayer. However, to the extent that the political solution is inconsistent with market forces, those protected by the government assistance will lobby to make the policies permanent, reducing incentives to adjust to world competitive conditions. Postponing required economic adjustments may in the end produce more painful and larger economic changes in the future, not to speak of the accumulated economic damage to users of products priced higher than world competitive levels. Industrial policy may have damaging effects to the extent that it prevents adjustment of an industry to develop new technology.

A renewed call for planning in the United States has been sounded with the name "industrial policy." This call is in response in large part to the major adjustments taking place in the traditional manufacturing sectors such as steel, automobiles, and textiles. The dislocations represented by persistent unemployment and corporate failures or recombinations in these industries are associated with the relocation of industrial power to regions with comparative cost advantages that may have resulted from rigidities induced by government regulation.

Any call for "industrial policy" that produces government interference in markets for affected products will have international trade implications. The serious issues raised by the interaction of "industrial policy" and international trade have not been at the center of the discussion that has hitherto been dominated by the need to rationalize the adjustment process. To explore these issues in an impartial academic surrounding, the School of Business of the University of Southern California held a conference in March 1984, on "Industrial Policy and International Trade." Some of the best known scholars in the country concerned with international trade issues prepared special papers or comments for the conference, and this volume represents the proceedings of that conference.

"Industrial Policy," we conclude, is not the answer to the adjustment problems of a few U.S. industries. The papers, comments of discussants, and discussion at the conference by and large reaffirm a pragmatic free trade view of the world in the industrial policy debate. However, trade interference will be difficult to avoid as interest groups choose to pursue government power over the marketplace as an arena for competition and protection of self-interest. There are interesting patterns and important differences between trade interventions by government policymakers in response to macroeconomic adjustments taking place through the balance of payments and microeconomic interventions in more narrowly defined markets affected by imports. Once in place, trade interventions may diffuse and make it difficult to identify costs to a complex economy like today's world economy. Restrictions on trade, however, have few of the desired effects, and turn creative economic energy toward avoiding, mitigating, or offsetting the effects of trade intervention. The lesson then is to be mindful of political realities which engender forces to move us farther from the optimal free trade world, in pursuit of continuing world economic growth and efficiency.

CONFERENCE OVERVIEW

The conference begins with a paper by Lee Price then of the United Auto Workers, "A Constructive Role for Government in the International Economy." The paper sets the agenda for the conference, as Price assures us that intervention in trade is inevitable, and that such intervention can be beneficial. Price reviews major recent economic developments, such as the oil embargo and the end of fixed exchange rates, and traces the history of government regulation of industries in response to these events. Price argues that rigidities in the economy together with the much larger impact of international events in domestic economic conditions mandate government assistance during transitions.

In the course of his paper, Price delineates conditions under which industrial policy is justified. Price argues that industrial policy should be used to restructure domestic factor and product markets. Trade policy is one instrument to support that restructuring. Rather than selective reactions such as voluntary export restraints (VER), Price advocates the establishment of a framework of planning and consultation under a new safeguards clause in the GATT.

Truman Clark, in his discussion of Price's paper, distills the issues raised by Price into a set of questions raised by advocacy of industrial policy that must be addressed. Among these are: Which industries will be revitalized; Who will make these determinations; and How should the costs of the policies be allocated? Clark concludes that, absent convincing answers to these questions, answers that account for economic efficiency and fairness (which he doubts can be made by advocates of industrial policy), market forces should be allowed to work.

The conference does not provide answers for all the questions Price and Clark raise, but it does begin the process by examining some of them. The questions raised by industrial policy in the form of trade intervention in an international economy can be roughly classified into two categories: the positive aspects and the normative aspects. Under the positive aspects, it is clear that trade intervention does occur, and the question is how and why such intervention takes place. The normative questions concern the costs and effectiveness of trade interventions.

Two papers examine positive issues concerning causes of trade intervention. Stephen P. Magee, Leslie Young, and William A. Brock focus on the political forces that result in protectionist policies. They analyze the nature of trade intervention in a theoretical model of a world with two factors, two goods, two lobbying groups, and two political parties that pursue their self-interests in terms of two policies, subsidies and tariffs. The contribution of their paper, "The Progressivity of Endogenous Tariff Policy in General Equilibrium," is in making tariffs and subsidies, which we can identify with industrial policy, an endogenous outcome in an economy with two factors of production.

In the Magee, Young, and Brock analysis, capital and labor both maximize their positions either through market activity or lobbying activity and under these very plausible model structures produce industrial policy. Their model explores the behavior of lobbies and political parties in the setting of commercial and industrial policy. Brock, Magee, and Young's analysis suggests that special interest groups use political pressure to force the government to intervene when competition from abroad threatens their industry. By contributing resources to their lobbying efforts, capital and labor may increase their incomes more through political action than through market competition.

Tim Campbell's discussion of the Magee, Young, and Brock paper is concerned with the property of rights of political parties or, as he describes them, sellers of persuasion. Political parties in the Brock, Young, and Magee model are owned by interest groups. The largest segment of the political system favors free trade yet owns no political party, otherwise they could win every election. In a more generally specified model, Campbell says, "there would be a market for persuasion, and political parties would not be owned by interest groups but would compete for resources." Campbell traces some complications of these observations in his discussion.

The second paper attempting to explain existing trade intervention is our paper, "Economic Determinants of U.S. Trade

Policy: An Empirical Analysis." An historical review of U.S. trade policy demonstrates that "fair trade" is not free trade. We estimate the actual quantitative relationships between recent policy actions affecting international trade and measures of interest group adjustment costs. Our empirical model links across-the-board trade restrictions to fluctuations in the U.S. trade balance representing wealth transfers abroad. However, we do not find a relation between across-the-board trade restrictions and domestic economic fluctuations in the form of unemployment and stock returns. We associate this pattern of policy responses to the trade balance with "neomercantilism."

On an industry by industry basis, however, labor and capital income effects measured by employment growth and industry stock returns have the most power in explaining trade restrictions at the commodity level. Surprisingly, growth in imports in affected industries does not figure significantly in explaining trade interventions. Our results are consistent with the theoretical model of Magee, Young, and Brock with respect to the behavior of special interest groups in the setting of industrial policy.

Tamir Agmon discusses some ramifications of our findings in his comments. Agmon is concerned about the linkages between political action and trade disturbances. In this respect, he finds the contrast between the results for across-the-board and individual industry results inconsistent and puzzling.

The preceding two papers address the issue of why and how much trade intervention we can expect in an economy with interest groups affected by international trade. The rest of the conference papers deal with the normative side of trade intervention. Ed Tower provides an innovative way to assess the distortions from trade intervention in a new equivalence theorem in his paper, "On the Symmetry Between Effective Tariffs and Value-Added Subsidies." Tower's primary theoretical contribution is to show that tariff policy is equivalent to a value-added subsidy for factors of production. This equivalence demonstrates the complex and often veiled effects of industrial policy in the form of tariffs on economic efficiency, since nontrade-affected industries factor returns will be affected by the implicit subsidies. Tower then discusses the key policy implication of his paper by showing how to set up an effective trade liberalizing scheme by restoring pre-intervention relative prices through value-added taxes. In his comments, Sebastian Edwards places Tower's work into the context of the effective protection literature in trade theory by showing how it fits into a taxonomy of trade restrictions.

A brief second paper by Ed Tower, Victor Canto, and William Kaempfer extends the equivalence between import and export taxes to an economy with nontraded, as well as internationally traded, goods. An implication of their analysis is that export promotion policies and import substitution policies, both elements of popular discussions of industrial policy, have the effect of offsetting each other. Despite this result, many countries simultaneously pursue both policies. Although there is no real effect on trade, the economy endures the distortion of the tax scheme used to finance and set up these programs.

The effectiveness of industrial policy is rarely questioned by its advocates, yet Gary Saxonhouse demonstrates in his paper, "Japanese High Technology, Government Policy, and Evolving Comparative Advantage in Goods and Services," that government policy has had little if any influence on the much renowned Japanese success in international competition. This paper uses statistical analysis of taxes, capital allocations, and case studies of industries to provide a detailed demonstration of the argument that, in fact, Japanese "industrial policy" really represents a set of uniquely Japanese institutions replacing more effective Western capital and labor markets and education and research establishments. The institutions and programs developed to overcome deficiencies in the Japanese economy hence followed, rather than promoted, basic economic developments in Japan.

Gerald Nickelsburg contends in his comment that Saxonhouse overstates his case that Japanese policy had no effect on Japanese economic growth since World War II. Nickelsburg provides a model of technology diffusion that suggests there are conditions of optimal subsidies that provide a backdrop against which to measure the actual practice in Japan described in Saxonhouse.

Our concluding round table discussion is captured in the paper by Arthur Laffer, "Trading Policy Outlook." Based on a detailed review of recent trade policy actions, Laffer argues for a free trade policy and is convinced that market forces in the end dominate economic outcomes in spite of recent protectionism. Trade policy or industrial policy at best result in costless bureaucratic actions, at worst impose adjustment and avoidance costs which outweigh any benefits to protected interests. Laffer advocates that the United States return to a leadership role in restoring the momentum of previous decades toward free trade world characterized by sustained economic expansion.

A CONSTRUCTIVE ROLE FOR GOVERNMENT IN THE INTERNATIONAL ECONOMY

Lee Price[1]

OVERVIEW

Most sectors of the U.S. economy are rapidly becoming more integrated into the world economy. Yet, as of 1984, decision making in the U.S. government remained almost totally oblivious to this trend. As long as foreign competition remained a peripheral matter for the bulk of our economy, we understandably ignored the trade effects of tax, spending, monetary, and regulatory decisions and relegated trade policy to bureaucratic enforcement against specific trade practices.

Debates over industrial policy generally resolve into a dispute between optimists and pessimists about the capacity of the U.S. government to carry out policies to deal with foreign economic rivalry. Many opponents of industrial policy tend to dismiss the concept as a smokescreen for trade restrictions or other industry giveaways. Others believe that, regardless of motivations, any conscious government concern for trade problems will amost necessarily deteriorate into the rationalization of inappropriate trade barriers.

Most proponents of industrial policy, on the other hand, are looking for less disruptive alternatives to deal with trade competition. They believe adoption of their approach would not increase either the propensity of the U.S. government to restrict trade or the degree of restrictions. That propensity will grow whether or not the government attempts a more coherent industrial policy. As this paper will show, the economic and political pressures for plain and simple trade restrictions are intensifying in any case. A sound industrial policy would result in fewer direct trade restrictions. It would defuse pressures for them in advance by providing alternatives. Where necessary, it would complement but mitigate trade restrictions.

Proponents of industrial policy tend to start with different assumptions than traditional trade economists on several key issues. The former tend to emphasize created factors of production, to believe that government can be as informed, forwardlooking, and flexible as the equally bureaucratic private sector, and to be concerned about instability and prolonged unemployment. On the other hand, traditional trade economists tend to emphasize geographically fixed factors, to believe government is naive, clumsy, and myopic, and to assume either full employment equilibrium or the existence of strong tendencies to restore it.

Policy on international economic matters tends to reflect the domestic policy framework. In recent years, the U.S. government has retreated from an activist set of measures for education, training, the environment, workplace safety, antitrust, and other domestic matters on the grounds that "the private sector knows better," or "would spend the money better." But, ironically, the United States has been interfering more regularly and extensively in international trade than ever before. Most of these interventions in trade are justified on the grounds that they are offsetting distortions created by the industrial policies of foreign government's. Not coincidentally, in none of these interventions has the government sought to ensure that U.S. industry take steps to become stronger during the period of the intervention.

This has created an inadvertent, unique blend of industrial policies for the United States: reactive measures in trade and international economic policy combined with heightened laissez-faire policies toward purely domestic product and labor markets. This paper argues that, if anything, the priorities should be the reverse: governmental policies should focus more on restructuring in domestic labor and product markets and use trade policy as one instrument to support that restructuring.

THE HISTORICAL BACKDROP

To a large extent, current U.S. trade problems stem from the past success of U.S. trade policy efforts. Spearheaded by U.S. initiatives, the General Agreement on Tariffs and Trade (GATT) has substantially reduced tariffs on trade imposed by major industrial nations. This has contributed to a remarkable expansion of world manufactures trade, from $82 billion in 1963 to $1057 in 1983, which, after adjusting for inflation, represents a 329 percent increase in volume (GATT, 1984, Appendix Table A1).

In addition to the GATT's role in reducing tariffs, the United States has promoted that institution to discourage industrial policy measures. The government elaborated its opposition to industrial policy from the lessons it drew from the 1930s—it has believed that most government interventions would not be economically sound, with costs to both the intervening nations and its trading partners. The 1983 "Economic Report of the President" states bluntly that such measures "hurt the country which adopts them as well as other countries" (pp. 60-61) and bring problems for relations between those countries. Thus, American policy has generally viewed industrial policy both as a negative-sum game and as a threat to peaceful international relations.

Two exceptions in U.S. industrial policy contrast with this approach to civilian manufacturing: agricultural and defense-related industries. In these two areas, the U.S. government has set a strongly interventionist example: funding and disseminating advanced research, lending stability to final demand, and even supervising the conditions and location of production. Due to its own policies in these two areas, the United States has been more tolerant of other countries' interventions.

The post war U.S. orthodoxy is coming under challenge for two reasons: industrial policies appear to be working for major competitors of the United States and current U.S. policy is not producing full employment, growth, and competitiveness for the United States. The experience of Japan and some of the newly industrialized countries (NIC) suggests that intervention can be quite successful in economic terms. Their growth rates for output and for many improvements in standards of living have been without historical precedent.

Equally important, the growing trade difficulties among U.S. manufacturing industries has kindled the debate on the efficacy of industrial policy. With the increasing integration of the world economy in trade and finance, the fortunes of most U.S. industries have become increasingly tied to their competitiveness with foreign manufacturers. The once wide technological edge of many U.S. industries has eroded or been eliminated (Price, 1985). As a result, imports represent a rising share of many U.S. product markets and U.S. exports of some products a decreasing share. Many of these industries employ large numbers of workers.

For the first time in the postwar era, the volume of world trade failed to increase for two consecutive years during 1982 and 1983. National governments were probably intervening to restrict imports more than before, but we must look elsewhere to find the major reasons for the decline in trade. The volume of trade depends on healthy and growing national economies, available and affordable international credit, and stable exchange rates. Economies around the world have not experienced such a serious slowdown, such high real interest rates, nor such unstable exchange rates since the Great Depression. To make matters worse, some major national economies reverted to the preKeynesian faith that government should abstain from countercyclical stimulus.

SOURCES OF TRADE INSTABILITY AND SURGES

Trade has become an important source of instability for national economies, Governments everywhere seek to dampen that instability. Economists recognize the benefits of stabilization elsewhere but they have underestimated the degree and costs of potential instability in trade.

Some trade has always taken place because different locations possess different natural conditions, such as resources or climate. Far more important in the case of manufactured goods—which comprise the bulk of trade today—are factors which are not fixed geographically, such as technology, labor skills, transportation and communication infrastructure, labor costs, credit costs, taxes, and political ties or other locations. Unlike resources such as climate, these are subject to rapid and substantial transformation by government or the private sector. As a result, countries can not only find a way to produce most traded goods locally, but can alter their costs quickly.

In a world where both relative costs and potential capacity can shift more rapidly, the possibility of import surges becomes far greater. Import surges can rapidly displace tens of thousands of workers and billions of dollars worth of equipment, forcing them into long term and often permanent unemployment. As Shinohara has pointed out, trade economists have generally ignored this phenomenon, and thus have failed to appreciate the economic logic of export restraints. (Shinohara, 1982: 109-119)

Several developments in the United States and world economy in the last decade have had seismic effects on the structure of costs in the international marketplace. These developments have abruptly shifted trade patterns, undermined confidence in the stability of world trade, and aggravated employment problems in the United States and elsewhere. These developments show no sign of abating.

The world trading system has undergone five institutional changes culminating in abrupt changes in the 1970s. First, the demise of fixed exchange rates has been followed by an era of volatile exchange rates. Second, events in oil markets led to a rapid price increase in 1973-74 and 1979-80. Third, competition on the basis of wages has become more prevalent with the equalization of other costs and spread of technology internationally. Fourth, governments have become more competitive in promoting specific industries as they jockey for strategic position in the international division of labor. Finally, transnational enterprises have grown dramatically, raising new institutional problems. The world has had previous experience with erratic exchange rates, steep price increases of specific commodities, policy-created competitive advantage, and transnational enterprises. However, each has played a qualitatively more significant role in U.S. and world economic developments over the last decade.

Exchange Rates and Volatile Capital Flows

From its inception more than a decade ago, the system of floating exchange rates has bobbed on some stormy seas. The U.S. dollar, the Japanese yen, and the British pound sterling have experienced particularly volatile swings. In fact, the read trade weighted value of each has, within periods no longer than two years, either risen or fallen over 25 percent (Williamson, 1985). Some are predicting continuing volatility in 1985-86 (Marris, 1985).

Such wide swings in a nation's exchange rate directly affect its industries' international competitiveness far more than anything they can do for themselves or traditional trade policy measures can offset. This plays havoc with those industries' decisions about the appropriate competitive response.

Stringent monetary and credit policies of the United States initiated the sharp rise in the dollar in 1980. The widening structural deficit in the federal budget since 1981 has also contributed to keeping real interest rates high in the United States. As a result, the United States has increasingly become a net exporter of bonds and a greater net importer of goods. The U.S. deficit in merchandise trade widened from $42.7 billion in 1982 to $123.3 billion in 1984, while the current account deficit slipped from a $9.2 billion deficit to a $101.6 billion deficit.

The U.S. manufacturing sector has been particularly hard hit. Between 1980 and 1984, the volume of U.S. manufactured exports declined 18 percent while manufactured imports soared 68 percent. A $12.4 billion surplus deteriorated to an $88.7 billion deficit, for a total swing of $101.1 billion. That four-year swing in the manufactured trade balance represented the equivalent of 15.4 percent of U.S. manufacturing value-added in 1984.

The sharp rise in the exchange rate of the dollar does not entirely account for the current slide in U.S. trade performance. Slower growth abroad and debt crises in major developing country markets also took their toll on U.S. trade, but they share some of the same origins with the high dollar value.

The United States is the world's "borrower of first resort." High U.S. real interest rates and the drain of credit from the rest of the world to the United States have raised rates, reduced the credit available abroad, slowed growth, and depreciated currencies. The developing countries have faced weakened export markets, high interest rates, and much more expensive dollars for debt repayment. Thus, the monetary and fiscal measures to reduce real interest rates would reduce the U.S. trade deficit not only by lowering the exchange rate of the dollar, but by improving growth rates abroad and easing the debt servicing burden of developing countries.

Oil Prices

As prices for oil and other forms of energy have fluctuated up and down, they have profoundly affected international trade and competitiveness in many industries. Energy costs represent a substantial part of the total costs of many products and of many nations' trade balances. Higher world oil prices changed trade competitiveness and led to trade responses, both in American export industries (e.g., aluminum to Japan, petrochemicals and synthetic fibers to Europe) and import-competing industries (e.g., autos from Japan and steel seamless tube pipe from Europe). As higher oil prices affected trade balances, they put pressure on exchange rates and led to more trade friction between the United States and trading partners. Oil-importing countries like Japan and Brazil scrambled for offsetting exports, while oil-rich United Kingdom and Mexico found competitiveness in their nonoil industries eroding and turned to subsidies and other measures to offset that effect. When oil prices declined, the effects were reversed, but no less profound for the United Kingdom and Mexico.

Wage-Based Competition

Competition on the basis of wage differentials is growing in importance. As other types of costs and technology have become more comparable among vying locations, wage differentials take on greater importance.

Although the gap between labor costs in the United States and in most other countries has narrowed substantially over the last two decades, the gap between U.S. labor costs and those of its "average" trading partner has narrowed little, if any. This seeming paradox derives from the fact that U.S. trade is growing more rapidly with countries with much lower wages than those with more comparable wages.

The newly industrializing countries (NICs) (e.g., Brazil, Hong Kong, Mexico, Singapore, South Korea, Spain, and Taiwan) have experienced growth in output and two-way trade that far exceeds that of the industrial market economies. Similarly, but less well-appreciated, Japan's labor costs remain far lower than those of any other country with comparable sophistication in product and production technology.[2] This has contributed greatly to Japan's striking success in the more technology-intensive industries previously dominated by the high-wage United States and northern European countries.

As the NICs and Japan have improved their technological capacities but found their export thrusts blunted, they have diversified their production and exports into many new industries. To assist diversification, their governments are taking an active role in underwriting investment risks (potential new barriers to exports are important risks in themselves). Hence, the problem industries for the United States and Europe are multiplying.

Changing Government-Business Relations

Government programs to assist specific industries and locations have a long history. However, competition in international product markets has put governments in competition to promote local production more than ever before. To reduce costs in specific industries, they stimulate investment, support research and development, train labor, build infrastructure, moderate wages, and apply a myriad of other measures to affect local costs. They have usually taken these measures more for domestic purposes than for international trade purposes. However, as national economies have become more diligent in reducing specific strategic costs relative to their trading partners. In addition, each nation has become more self-conscious about how to structure its economy to fit into the world economy.

Two types of industry have received the most government assistance in OECD countries. The first type, those with stiff import competition and employment far too large to be moved readily into other production, now includes textiles apparel, steel, shipbuilding, and automobiles, among others. This category will no doubt expand if unemployment remains high, taking credibility from the argument that "workers can move into other industries." The second type includes those considered "high value-added," that is, that promise high profits and high wages: segments of electronics, telecommunications, aerospace, and others. The number of industries within this category could eventually shrink if countries do not take cognizance of each other's parallel actions. They may overbuild capacity to the point where some industries would become "low value-added" because of stiff price competition in the marketplace.

Targeting for future development is another form of industrial aid. The main assistance here has been in the form of government coordination, and even subsidization, of research and development, capital formation, and industrial development strategies. These programs—such as Japanese development of large scale integrated circuits or French development of telecommunications or the Defense Department's funding of large scale computer development in the United States—often do not have an immediate impact on trade, but may over a longer period. The government role may be negligible by the time the industry becomes internationally competitive and begins to export. Because of the lag in time and change in magnitude between the "targeted" assistance acorn and the mighty oak of foreign competition, U.S. subsidies legislation cannot effectively counter these policies.

Transnational Enterprises

Transnational enterprises (TNEs) have been producing similar products in many countries for a long time. In the early stages of their development, U.S. TNEs generally exported parts for assembly in host countries and imported few products back that were also manufactured here. In recent years, however, more and more TNEs have shifted production abroad and created a global web of integrated production. Their U.S. net positive trade balance has therefore been steadily eroding. These shifts in production location often represent a variant of the two previous items, low-wage competition and competing government policies. However, the TNEs deserve separate attention because (1) their transnational status accords them greater bargaining strength vis-à-vis employees and governments since they can threaten to shift more production abroad to get lower wages or more government assistance; (2) their control of marketing channels and technology often gives them autonomy over a considerable range to decide the location of production; and, (3) as centralized institutions with intimate knowledge of many national markets, they speed up the flow of production and technology to other countries, accelerating the product cycle from exports to production abroad.

After the experience of the last decade, few would predict long-term stability in exchange rates or oil prices, less foreign competition on the basis of wage differences, reduced intervention by foreign governments to enhance their industries' competitiveness, or a decline in TNE leverage. On the contrary, except perhaps for oil prices, these chronic and pervasive structural problems show every sign of growing in the years ahead.

IMPLICATIONS FOR DOMESTIC ECONOMIC CONDITIONS

These new structural conditions brought on by the deepened ties of the United States to the world economy complicate the management of U.S. macroeconomic policy. First, higher levels of trade reduce the efficacy of demand-oriented policies to stimulate the economy (which U.K. policymakers have recognized for some time). The higher the import share in total demand, the greater the "leakage" when the "pump is primed." In other words, the same increase in demand today brings a lower boost (macromultipler) to domestic production than it did when trade was less significant. Moreover, the higher demand for imports causes a shift in the trade balance which may depreciate the currency and spur inflation.

The twin problems of reduced macromultiplier and depreciating currency plagued the demand-stimulus effort of the Mitterrand government, increased the appeal of import restrictions in many countries, and encouraged others to promote simultaneous stimuli among the major industrial countries. Due to its greater borrowing power, the powerful U.S. fiscal stimulus after 1981 was more effective longer but eventually succumbed to substantial leakage. In the first quarter of 1985, U.S. demand grew at a strong 4.4 percent annual rate, but its GNP grew at an anemie 1.3 percent rate.

Second, Keynes also emphasized the "accelerator" linkage between investment and growth, the importance of "animal spirits" or persons making decisions for productive investment. Although the effects are difficult to quantify, substantially increased foreign competition has increased the uncertainty of investment decision makers. Their uncertainty has grown not only with the significance of foreign competition, but with volatility of exchange rates.

Third, the expansion of trade also tends to shift the distribution of jobs and income. The international marketplace pits products in competition with each other and, at one step removed, the workers who make them. Foreign competition can adversely affect not only those who lose their jobs, but also, those who must accept lower pay to keep their jobs. Less skilled workers in industrial countries are finding competitive imports put downward pressure on their jobs and wages. By the same token, other workers enjoy upward pressure of their wages when their skills are used in expanding export products or merchandising imports. The divergent effect on pay scales of the traded-goods sector spreads to comparably skilled workers in the rest of the economy.

Proponents of expanded trade correctly point out that U.S. products compete more successfully in international markets in which extensive skills and advanced technology are crucial. According to standard trade theory, the nation can "gain" from expanding these exports and importing more products made with fewer skilled workers and less standardized technology. However, expanded trade means more U.S. jobs and higher pay for workers with certain skills and *fewer* U.S. jobs and lower pay for other workers.

In the jousting over trade policy in the political arena, the differential effect of trade on occupations is causing new lines to be drawn. Political conflicts over basic trade policy once pitted the South, with its agricultural exports, versus the North, with its struggling manufacturing. In more recent times, the distinction between agriculture and manufacturing has become blurred and new lines have been drawn between more narrow export- and import-competing industries in both sectors. Now, particularly in industries with transnational enterprises, the clash occurs between less skilled production workers on the one hand, and more skilled or more strategically placed headquarters workers on the other.

The naive trade economists' notion of the U.S. as capital abundant and labor scarce has a spurious implication for the employment policy needed for expanded trade. Since trade is forcing less skilled workers into unemployment, we should be expanding resources for training, not contracting them.

Finally, the very process of integrating the national economy into the international economy involves increased economic specialization on the part of all national economies. This means that some industries expand in response to new export demand or become more competitive with imports while others contract in response to import competition or loss of export markets. This adjustment and integration process is not smooth or continuous. Moreover, it is frequently coupled with technological change, so that the newly competitive industries demand higher skills and employ fewer workers relative to new value-added. The net affect of the changes in trade and technology is that many jobs become outmoded and the nation's labor requirements fall (if growth is slow or zero). Moreover, the export industries often grow up in different regions than the industries with declining employment. This makes it all the more important than trade policy be integrated into a broader domestic strategy to restructure industry and labor and pursue rapid growth.

THE FOUNDATION OF U.S. TRADE POLICY

United States trade policy has historically been founded on two premises that, while not necessarily inconsistent with a self-conscious restructuring strategy, seem to work against the adoption of such programs. First, in U.S. eyes, the objective of international trading rules was the limitation of government interventions and preventing "distortion" of market processes. The U.S.-inspired postwar trading regime codified this principle. U.S. trade policy was the offsetting of distortions introduced into trade by other governments. This has resulted in an extensive body of law and litigative procedures designed solely to determine whether foreign governments have violated principles the United States considered to be embodied in the GATT.

However well these premises have served the United States in the past, the events described in the forgoing section limit their usefulness to achieve national goals such as full employment and sustained growth in times of global structure shifts. It is clear that they need to be supplemented with an approach to trade that integrates U.S. external policy more tightly with domestic policy. If the general posture of policy is not to intervene in home markets and to intervene in tradable goods markets only if other governments do, the government is constrained from adopting policies to promote change at home and left only with the threat of quasiprotectionist reprisal as the instrument to cope with international economic change. The debate over trade policy is then quickly cast as free trade versus protectionism, rather than as adjusting to economic change. Let us elaborate briefly on the traditional U.S. approach to GATT and to trade intervention.

The United States in the GATT: Proponent of Limited Government

From the earliest postwar negotiations through the GATT Ministerial in 1982, the United States has persisted in its efforts to restrict key elements of interventionist policies such as subsidies, government procurement, and restrictions on investment. The GATT was written as a set of provisional rules to backstop the 1947 round of multilateral tariff negotiations. Related negotiations over the International Trade Organization (ITO) charter began the year before and were completed the following year. The GATT rules were initially intended primarily to prevent countries from using nontariff measures to nullify the effect of their new tariff cuts until the full ITO charter came into effect. The ITO itself never got off the ground because the U.S. Congress would not agree to join.

The drafting of the GATT rules and the stillbirth of the ITO reflect U.S. efforts and frustrations in reshaping the world to accept minimalist government intervention. When negotiations began for the GATT and the ITO charter, the United States presented draft documents that formed the basis of discussions. The United States proposed strict rules to limit nontariff devices to curb imports or promote exports (e.g., subsidies, government procurement, quotas during balance of payments difficulties) with vigorous legal adjudication of alleged violations.

Most of the rest of the world has never accepted the U.S. position on the proper role of government. By the time the final documents were signed, other countries had succeeded in adding or expanding many exceptions to the restraints on government intervention. These exceptions became a focal point for U.S. critics of the ITO. Because of the unwillingness of the United States and other governments to surrender sovereignty to an international organization, no effective dispute settlements procedures were adopted. Most disputes that have arisen under the GATT have been resolved by negotiation and compromise, rather than adjudication. This approach has effectively sanctioned many technical violations of the GATT (Jackson 1969, pp. 35-37; Dam, 1970, pp. 12-16).

The performance of the GATT over the last three decades has far exceeded the role initially expected of it as a mere backstop to the 1947 tariff cuts. However, its role has been far less extensive than that envisioned for the ITO. Under GATT auspices, seven "rounds" of multilateral trade negotiations have been conducted. These negotiations have succeeded in greatly reducing tariffs on manufactured goods among industrialized member countries. In addition, the last two rounds resulted in codes covering nontariff issues in trade.

Multilateral negotiations have provided a political dynamic that has been conducive to nondiscriminatory liberalization. In particular, they mobilize political activity on a broad spectrum of export interests. These groups, in turn, pressure their nation's representatives to negotiate lower foreign tariffs and to accept domestic tariff cuts. Since domestic constituencies measure success in mercantilist terms, a government can justify making tariff "concessions" only by showing foreign tariff reductions for products it exports. With many countries involved, more reductions can be shown to "the folks back home." Lastly, governments more readily accept tariff cuts being applied on a nondiscriminatory basis if all their major trading partners are simultaneously reciprocating with a package of comparable cuts. (Each country's package of cuts involves different products.)

The Tokyo Round from 1973 to 1979 marked the first time in GATT's seven rounds of negotiations in which as much attention was devoted to curbing nontariff barriers as to reducing tariffs. The Round further exemplifies U.S. resistance to industrial policy measures. As its top two priorities, the United States sought "codes" to restrict the use of subsidies and to grant national treatment in government procurement, issues on which it had been forced to compromise when the GATT was first written. Advocates of industrial policy, on the other hand, often recommend using these practices for national advantage.

The Subsidies Code, the highest priority of the United States in the Tokyo Round, prohibits export subsidies on nonprimary products by industrial countries and permits a country to counteract a foreign governments' domestic subsidies in Europe or less developed countries. The code has, however, provided the

United States with justification to take more vigorous action against subsidized imports from those areas.

The Government Procurement Code forbids discrimination against imported goods for contracts over 150,000 Special Drawing Rights (approximately US $150,000) for a set of products and/or government agencies specified by each country. A thorough empirical analysis of this code has not yet been made public. However, preliminary evidence suggests that the code has had very modest effects.

One can draw the following conclusion from the U.S. attempts in GATT to negotiate government intervention out of the market place: First, GATT has been overwhelmingly successful in reducing barriers to trade that meet three criteria: tariffs, for manufactured goods, by industrial countries, but it has had very limited success elsewhere. Second, the new wave of industrial policies and increased business-government coordination falls largely outside the GATT and, for the foreseeable future, will remain undisciplined by international accord.

The United States at Home: Defender Against Foreign Governments

United States trade officials have shown their antipathy toward industrial policy measures not only in international negotiations but in domestic policy toward imports. The U.S. government far more readily restricts imports to offset some "unfair" foreign action than to relieve domestic injury caused by imports. As a practical matter, industrial policy measures abroad comprise most of the actions that American trade officials consider "unfair."

When the U.S. government intervenes in trade in an attempt to offset foreign government measures, it does so on the grounds that it is defending "free but fair trade." Giving help to the domestic industry may motivate the government, but the overriding public rationale is to make import prices what they hypothetically would have been without specific government interventions.

In recent years, as enforcement of "fair trade" laws against subsidies and other "unfair" practices has expanded, the law to regulate imports solely on the basis of injury to the domestic industry has languished (Section 201 of the 1974 Trade Act implements the "Escape Clause," Article XIX of the GATT). This is unfortunate, for when relief is granted, it should preferably be tailored to the conditions of the domestic industry which Section 201 permits but the fair trade laws do not. Section 201 requires that, before relief is granted, the petitioning industry must submit its plans for adjustment to international competition. Moreover, in theory Section 201 permits imports to be restrained to the extent and for the period (up to 8 years) necessary to relieve injury. This contrasts with relief under the "fair trade" laws, which make no provision for action to be taken by the domestic industry and for which the degree and duration of restraint is based on the unfair foreign practice.

Petitions for import relief under Section 201 have declined for both legal and political reasons. United States law has a tougher legal requirement than the GATT. GATT Article XIX requires only that imports cause "serious injury." However, Section 201 does not permit import relief when the injury from any other source exceeds serious import injury. In the auto case of 1980, it was decided that imports caused such injury, but that a general decline in sales constituted an even greater single source of injury. As a result, the test for Section 201 relief can seldom be proved by a cyclically sensitive industry during a recession.

A major political hurdle confronts an industry that can convince the International Trade Commission (ITC) that it meets the legal standards of Section 201. Even if the ITC recommends that relief be granted to the petitioning industry, complete discretion rests with the President to decide whether to grant relief and, if so, what form it should take. Tipping the scales against granting relief is the requirement for "compensation" to exporting countries (discussed more fully in the discussion of safeguards below) and diplomatic concerns vis-à those countries.

In comparison to Section 201, industries have found petitions for relief against subsidized imports far more attractive, particularly since 1979 (Jackson, 1985). Once subsidies are shown, the law requires proof of only nominal injury, if at all. Administration discretion not to enforce the law vigorously is seldom, if ever, invoked (at least since the Department of Commerce assumed responsibility from the Treasury in 1979). Since the GATT rules do not require compensation for actions against subsidized imports, the Administration has less reluctance to restrict them.

As a result of the 1969 Subsidies Code, U.S. subsidies law now permits a quota to be imposed as a remedy for subsidized imports. Previously, the only available remedy had been countervailing duties (CVD) equal in value to the subsidies. This change laid the basis for the 1982 settlement with the EEC for a three-year restraint of their carbon steel exports. That case, and the 1984 steel case, highlight the problem of the rise of subsidies law and fall of Section 201. When an unfair foreign subsidy is isolated as causing injury, a CVD seems the appropriate remedy. However, if a quota affecting a third (1982) or virtually all (1984) of steel imports is going to be administered a thorough examination should be conducted of the domestic industry and some assurance should be forthcoming about a stronger domestic industry in the end. Despite the best efforts of the steelworkers union and the 1984 trade legislation, no such assurance was secured.

Section 301 petitions of the USTR represent another increasingly popular avenue against foreign government actions. That section gives the President rather open-ended power to retaliate against vaguely defined "unfair" foreign actions. The many versions of so-called reciprocity legislation proposed in the last few years essentially seek to widen the scope and/or increase the leverage of this provision. In practice, American politicians tend to consider "unfair" those measures used abroad which are more restrictive of U.S. businesses than U.S. measures. In effect, the United States uses the yardstick of its own domestic measures to judge the validity of foreign measures.

As a practical matter, substantial subsidies and other government interventions have become commonplace for many of our trading partners. Since they seem unlikely to scale these practices back to any significant degree, we can expect many more successful petitions to restrict imports on the basis of "free but fair" trade.

"VOLUNTARY" EXPORT RESTRAINTS

Voluntary export restraints (VERs) have become an increasingly popular prescription to ease the perceived pain of import competition. They have been used most commonly to prevent damaging surges in vulnerable and politically organized industries (e.g., televisions, shoes, steel, autos). In the most recent VERs negotiated in both carbon and specialty steel, however, the official rationale was simply to counter unfair foreign trade practices, not to relieve domestic injury.

Economists have tended to dismiss VERs as another form of unwarranted quota and not acknowledged their distinctive characteristics. VERs have generally been obtained by stronger countries seeking relief while avoiding the cost of compensation or the risk of retaliation provided by GATT rules. According to GATT Article XIX, before a country may raise barriers to imports causing injury, it must consult all countries who are exporting the product to it (except in an emergency). It may "compensate" those exporters by agreeing on reductions of barriers to other products it buys from them. If no agreement is reached, the exporting countries may "retaliate" by raising barriers to imports of comparable value from the noncompensating country within ninety days.

Exporting countries bow to VERs for several reasons. In contrast to tariffs, the exporting country is assured of reaping all the scarcity rents from its restricted supply. In contrast to restrictions unilaterally imposed by the importing country, VERs are more likely to be adjusted and possibly even removed over time (witness the Japanese auto restraints).

Japan has agreed to place more of its exports under VERs than any other country. Hence, a resolution on VERs adopted by the powerful Japanese business federation Keidanren in February 1985 has particular significance. The resolution provides their rationale for VERs and the conditions under which they are willing to accept GATT sanction for them.

> Voluntary export restraints and other bilateral arrangements contradict the spirit of GATT, which is free, nondiscriminatory, and multilateral. We must not have easy recourse to such steps.

> On occasion bilateral measures may be adopted when, for example, a sharp rise in exports of a particular type threatens severe damage to an import industry of a trading partner—in the long-term interest of preserving free trade by resolving problems before they worsen and turn into political issues. We must facilitate the removal of such restraints, however, when the protected industry shows signs of recovery. For this purpose, it should be required that countries taking such measures notify GATT and place the measures under GATT supervision, making clear the basis on which they are implemented and limiting their duration, and that the importing country take steps for industrial adjustment. Such a process should improve the transparency of these measures. This is one of the important issues to be discussed at a new round of trade negotiations.
>
> Meanwhile, individual corporations must also take care that their exports are orderly so as not to upset world markets. (Keidanren, 1985)

These Keidanren guidelines adopted in 1985 run remarkably parallel to those suggested below which this author had proposed at the 1984 USC conference.

THE OPPORTUNITY PROVIDED BY THE SAFEGUARDS CODE

Negotiation of a Safeguards Code would offer an opportunity to begin developing some internationally agreed upon principles that would be applicable to national industrial policies. The Safeguards Code would provide rules for imposing import restrictions. The most important issues applicable to industrial policies are the conditions for granting import relief, consultation treatment of other countries, and transparency with international monitoring of actions taken. Unfortunately, the very troubling conflicts between competitive industrial policies also come on the export side, both into competitors' home markets and into third-country markets. Policies that promote industries for export go beyond the reach of a Safeguards Code.

The Safeguards Code should include incentives against the imposition of import restraints in the absence of a program for domestic restructuring of the protected industry. That would, of course, entail a shift in U.S. trade policy. In the few times import relief has been granted by the United States, the government has not sought commitments from domestic firms to restructure to become a stronger industry. Too frequently, industries have squandered the respite and additional revenues coming from import relief. For example, during a succession of measures restraining steel imports, the U.S. steel companies have diversified out of steel production and into other industries. Likewise, as primarily small cars from Japan have been limited, U.S. auto companies have shifted out of U.S. small car production and/or production of small cars abroad.

All significant new restrictions on imports should be accompanied by a careful assessment of the industry's trade difficulties and, unless the problems appear transitory, a plan for restructuring. The assessment should include an inventory of the capacity and key characteristics of all domestic facilities, a comparison of the technology in place with the world's best-practice technology, and an evaluation of all costs of production, including equipment, materials, management staffing, and labor. The restructuring plan for a protected industry should seek to achieve the benefits otherwise available from open trade, in terms of competitive pressures on product design and cost reduction through production technology, scale economies, and so on. Such restructuring may include acquiring, developing, and disseminating best-practice technology, upgrading the skills of workers, phasing out facilities that cannot be renovated, and cutting unjustified costs. Where jobs are displaced, workers should be retrained, preferably for jobs in the same vicinity. At the same time, the restructuring effort should promote competition within the domestic industry. In some cases, restructuring might involve an upgrading of some facilities but a gradual scaling back of industry capacity; in others it might entail maintaining capacity and include some new facilities.

Consultation is a second concern. Countries have legitimate concerns about their trading partners' policies to improve the competitiveness of local industry. This holds true whether the industrial policy at issue tends to counter imports (where the Safeguards Code would apply), to promote exports, or both. When an industrial policy is implemented, other countries with competing industries should have the rights to full information about the extent of government assistance to each industry and to consultation over its effects. If done properly, this kind of exchange can accomplish a number of positive results. If the two governments better understand each other's problems, they can shape their respective policies to reduce conflicts and ultimately accept the results with less rancor. They can try to avoid squandering funds on offsetting subsidies. Finally, over time they could learn from each other's experience.

As noted above, GATT members have honored the applicable "Escape Clause" rules for import relief consultations more in the breach than in practice. In practice, powerful countries have been achieving import relief without paying compensation or suffering retaliation. They have used their leverage to obtain either "voluntary" export restraints or acquiescence to unilateral import barriers.

The leverage to coerce "voluntary" restrains has depended in part on the absence of transparency in obtaining them. Transparency is therefore a third issue. Concerns for the continued favorable treatment of its own exports circumscribes the actions that a country is willing to take against imports. Every government watches the policies taken toward its exports by its trading partners. A country's propensity to shelter its industries can be offset by the fear that such actions would be used to justify foreign actions against its exports. However, if a country can secretly restrain imports, it avoids such inhibitions.

Transparency thus provides some disincentive even if it is much weaker than that provided by the Escape Clause's right of retaliation. Due to the importance and vulnerability of its exports, no country can openly depart very far from the norms of its trading partners in carrying out import relief for its industries.

Transparency is not the rule today. Trading partners regularly uncover secret arrangements by other countries to restrict imports. Some countries, particularly France and Japan, have often been accused of substantial covert import restrictions. The absence of transparency arouses suspicion among trading partners and creates an atmosphere in which mutual confidence in the continued openness of trade declines. On the other hand, self-restraining in erecting import barriers would be reinforced by greater transparency, that is, it countries felt more fully informed about the import restraints of their trading partners.

Negotiations for a Safeguards Code foundered during the Tokyo Round and current discussions about a new GATT round have attempted to revive them. In 1979, impasse developed over the issue of "selectivity"—the restriction of imports from some but not all source countries. Selectivity violates the nondiscrimination principle of GATT Article I. Governments have proposed rules that would effectively sanction their own current practices. The European Community wanted a sanction to restrict imports on a selective basis unilaterally; the United States also favored selectivity, but on a "consensual basis," that is, with the agreement of the exporting country; finally, Japan and the developing countries opposed any code that would sanction discriminatory import restrictions.

GATT members could adopt a Safeguards Code that emphasized transparency, but remained silent with respect to selectivity. For the code to have any practical value, it must have the signature of the European Community and the United States, both of whom insist on the freedom to apply selective import restrictions. If the code is silent on selectivity, those who oppose it in the code could continue to resist it. They can argue that, as part of the GATT structure, the code is subject to the nondiscrimination principles of GATT Article I. The Keidanren statement quoted above suggests that Japan may be willing to move on this issue.

To achieve success with the goal of "transparency," the safeguards code should cover all import restraints even selective ones, informal ones, and actions against subsidies, dumping, and other "unfair" trade practices. These restraints should be reported to and monitored by the GATT. To work effectively, the code must include some form of sanction for failure to report restraints. Otherwise, countries restraining imports will continue to enforce silence.

CONCLUSION

The decline in the relative competitiveness of many of its manufacturing industries makes the U.S. government prone to take actions to prop up domestic production in specific industries. Sustained and robust world growth is problematic and could alleviate only some of the problems of specific industries and tensions between countries. Continued problems with exchange rates, energy costs, low wage competition, competitive government intervention, and TNE pressure will make government interventions ever more attractive.

Actions taken at the border that are directed solely at foreign competitors have obvious political appeal. For that reason, restrictive trade measures could become the sum and substance of a future "industrial policy" this would be most unfortunate. Typically, the economic conditions which compel import restraints also can justify industry- (and even company-) specific intervention, to restructure industry capacity with best-practice technology throughout, retrain those workers where there has been outmoded capacity—preferably for jobs at the same location, and attract new industries into regions with a loss of jobs. To achieve these goals for either a growth industry or a distressed industry, merely granting relief from imports (as well as taxes and regulations) will not suffice. Instead, the U.S. government must, on the one hand, promote restructuring with industry negotiations, possibly accompanied by training, subsidies, government purchases, and regulation of investment. On the other hand, it must seek multilateral rules to regulate industrial policies to avoid injury to trading partners; at the same time, the United States should pursue international consultations to resolve differences over industrial policies.

The alternative to a recognition on the part of the U.S. government that its trade policy must support a vigorous restructuring effort is to maintain the debate as one of free trade versus protectionism. The choice should not be between "free trade"—that is, a policy of no government action in trade-related markets-and "protectionism"—simply holding back imports from the U.S. market. This gives threatened workers and businesses no recourse but to choose protection. As it stands, if protection is granted, it is not linked to a program of renewal; the protection either builds a constituency for itself or firms eventually adjust through diversification or captive imports while workers are left to fend for themselves. Ironically, too often the political outcome is quasipermanent import barriers in the name of free trade.

If protection is not granted and serious injury occurs to domestic industry, displaced workers bear the brunt of the adjustment process without recourse to retraining programs. Society at large must pay the external costs of unemployment, including the direct costs of unemployment, related taxes foregone, and additional benefits paid, as well as the indirect costs of higher rates of suicide, divorce, and violence.

If the buildup of economic pressures is making some form of interventionism more likely, the political consequences for the United States are not at all clear. In response to the economic crisis of the 1930s, fundamental shifts in political structures accompanied the profound change in the relationship between business, labor, and national governments of the United States and Europe. At that time, the United States enjoyed a resurgence of democratic institutions, particularly the organization of workers in the growth industries of the era. On the other hand, Germany and Italy enjoyed some economic success but at a terrible cost in the weakening of their democratic institutions.

Negotiation of international norms to reduce conflicts between national industrial policies must await U.S. recognition of the legitimacy of certain forms of interventionist policies. Until then, negotiations over the Safeguards Code can preliminarily address an important common element: transparency of—and consultation over—the plan of adjustment.

In summary, the U.S. government faces a formidable set of challenges: to strengthen our democratic institutions, to avoid the demagoguery of blaming foreigners for problems that should be resolved domestically, to recognize the efficacy and legitimacy of trade measures as part of an economically sound restructuring policy, and to negotiate agreements to mitigate the international conflicts that arise due to competing industrial policies.

NOTES

1. This paper was written for a conference in early 1984 with minor revisions in 1985 when the author was an economist for the International Union, United

Automobile, Aerospace, and Agricultural Implement Workers (UAW). The arguments made herein do not represent the views of the UAW or the author's subsequent employers, nor are they the arguments that he would make on behalf of an industrial policy in 1992.

2. The Bureau of Labor Statistics has made provisional estimates for the total hourly labor costs for production workers in manufacturing in 1984. With the U.S. labor cost indexed at 100, other advanced industrial countries ranged as follows: Japan—50, United Kingdom—46, Italy—58, France—60, Belgium—70, Sweden—72, Germany—75, and Canada—90. (Bureau of Labor Statistics, 1985).

REFERENCES

Bureau of Labor Statistics: Office of Productivity and Technology. 1985. "Hourly Compensation Cost for Production Workers in Manufacturing, 34 Countries, 1975-84." Unpublished data. Washington, D.C.: Bureau of Labor Statistics.

Council of Economic Advisors. 1983. *Economic Report of the President.*

Dam, Kenneth. 1970. *The GATT: Law and International Economic Organization.* Chicago: University of Chicago Pres.

General Agreement on Tariffs and Trade. 1984. *International Trade 1983/84* Geneva.

Jackson, John H. 1969. *World Trade and the Law of GATT.* Indianapolis: Bobbs Merrill.

Jackson, John H. 1985. *Trade Action Inventory.* East Lansing: University of Michigan Law School.

Keidanren. 1985. "Toward Rebuilding and Strengthening the Free-Trade System." Keizai Koho Center, *KKC Brief* No. 27.

Marris, Stephen. 1985. *Dollars and Deficits: the World Economy at Risk.* Washington, DC: Institute for International Economics.

Price, Lee. 1985. "Growing Problems for American Workers in International Trade," in *Challenges and Choices Facing American Labor,* ed. Thomas A. Kochan. Cambridge, MA: MIT Press.

Shinohara, Miyohei. 1982. *Industrial Growth, Trade, and Dynamic Patterns in the Japanese Economy.* Tokyo: University of Tokyo Press.

Williamson, John. 1985. *The Exchange Rate System.* Washington, DC: Institute for International Economics.

COMMENT ON "A CONSTRUCTIVE ROLE FOR GOVERNMENT IN THE INTERNATIONAL ECONOMY"

Truman A. Clark

TRADE ISSUES IN U.S. INDUSTRIAL POLICY

In recent years, major American industries (such as steel and automobile manufacturing) have been forced to reduce their levels of production due to their inability to compete effectively with imported goods. Since these industries employ large numbers of workers, their retrenchment has resulted in the loss of the jobs of many American laborers. What should the United States do about this problem?

An answer to this question is presented in the paper by Lee Price. Mr. Price does not believe that the United States should remain passive and allow the fates of major industries and their workers to be determined solely by market forces. Instead, he calls for the development of an "industrial policy" for the planned reorganization of this nation's ailing industries under the aegis of a "Safeguard's Code." Price, in his verbal presentation, asserted that certain infirm industries should be targeted for revitalization.

Large investments in these industries would be encouraged to insure the use of the most advanced technology and modern facilities and equipment. Government is expected to assist in this restoration process by granting selected subsidies and tax cuts.

During the period required to complete their revitalization, Price believes that the chosen industries will require a respite from the rigors of unrestricted import competition. Thus, he proposes the use of "temporary" protectionist measures to shield these industries until they are restored to full competitive strength.[1]

Mr. Price also recognizes that there are some industries which must be scaled down. In such industries, and in others where the adoption of new technology reduces the need for labor, Price is concerned about the plight of workers who lose their jobs. Displaced workers bear large personal costs, and Mr. Price believes that it is society's responsibility to reduce these costs to tolerable levels. To accomplish this, Mr. Price proposes that the government provide the training necessary so that displaced workers can qualify for new jobs.

The paper by Lee Price serves as a useful introduction to this conference on industrial policy and international trade. It expresses views which are held by many people in organized labor, corporate management, and government policy-making positions. It also raises a number of important issues upon which this conference will focus. Several of these issues are identified in the questions which I would like to raise concerning the industrial policy outlined by Lee Price.

1. *Why are a number of American industries currently in dire conditions?*

Lee Price offers some suggestions (e.g., floating exchange rates, fluctuating energy prices, and the success of the industrial policies adopted by the governments of other countries), but I believe there are more fundamental causes which Mr. Price overlooks. Past and current government actions (e.g., overregulation, excessive taxes, and import restrictions to shield domestic industries from foreign competition) are partly to blame. In many cases, management has also been derelict in responding to foreign competition, for instance, American automobile manufacturers have been very reluctant to design and produce smaller model cars to compete with cars imported from Japan. Finally, by contributing to the wide wage disparities between American and foreign labor markets, labor unions in the United States are also partly responsible for the decline in the competitive positions of many domestic industries.

2. *Who will decide which industries will be revitalized and which will be scaled down?*

In his paper, Mr. Price does not provide an answer to this question, but I assume he believes that government officials, corporate executives, and union leaders should share in the decision making. If my assumption is correct, Mr. Price wants the same enlightened groups which have gotten many American industries into their current predicaments to come together and use their collective wisdom to straighten things out.

3. *How will the choices concerning the restructuring of American industries be made?*

Under the proposal of Lee Price, the invited parties will meet and hammer out deals. In return for import restrictions that will save some jobs, unions must agree to limit future wage demands. In return for subsidies and tax breaks, management must commit to major investment programs to upgrade domestic productivity. While the special interests of corporate management and organized labor will be represented in the meetings where such deals are struck, how will more general interests be protected? The agreements between government, management, and organized labor are likely to impose costs on consumers, taxpayers, and nonunion labor, but these latter groups will not be represented in the councils where the deals are made.

4. *Who benefits from and who bears the costs of an industrial policy and import restrictions?*

In democratic countries, it is in the self-interest of politicians to confer benefits which are highly visible while imposing costs which are nearly indetectable. For this reason, Lee Price's plan will undoubtedly appeal to many politicians.

The benefits of the Lee Price proposal would be highly concentrated. The main beneficiaries would be the workers and managers whose jobs are saved and, possibly, the shareholders of firms in the industries chosen for temporary protection and overhaul.

The costs of the plan would be widely spread. The imposition of import restrictions would harm consumers by restricting their choices, raising prices, and reducing the quality of goods available. Import restrictions would also reduce the number of dollars foreigners have with which to purchase American goods, and also invite retaliation against American exports. Both of these results would work to reduce American exports and thereby harm our export industries and their workers. Subsidies and other forms of financial assistance to selected firms and worker groups involve transfers from other economic units; thus, they impose costs on taxpayers.

However, the damages an industrial policy and trade restrictions are likely to do to the American economy are of even greater importance. Under the industrial policy proposed by Lee Price, investment decision making is thrust into the political arena. Instead of being decided by private assessments of risk and return, investment choices are made for political gain, and thus largely determined by relative bargaining skills, lobbying, logrolling, and clout. In the interest of creating or saving a few jobs, it is highly likely that large, wasteful investment projects will be undertaken. The economy is clearly harmed if scarce capital resources are allocated to inferior investment opportunities. In addition, the trade restrictions proposed by Lee Price would reduce competition. Economic efficiency is lost whenever competition is reduced.

5. *Why should temporary protection from import competition be granted to reorganizing industries?*

Apparently, Lee Price believes that without such protection American industries cannot or will not make necessary changes. However, it is the pressure of competition which dictates that changes required to improve efficiency must be made quickly. Import restrictions reduce the incentive to make required changes, and the danger exists that firms in protected industries will institute changes at a slower pace and become even less efficient relative to foreign competitors. The pace of change in protected industries is likely to be especially slow if industrialists believe that a lack of progress can be used to argue for extensions of the "temporary" restrictions.[2]

Thus, it is important to recognize that the granting of temporary protection is risky. While some jobs may be saved temporarily, it is possible that an industry shielded from foreign competition will become relatively less efficient. If this occurs and the protection is finally lifted, the entire industry may be swept away with the permanent loss of all the jobs it provides.

6. *How much and what type of assistance should be granted to displaced workers?*

In answering the first part of this question, a trade-off must be recognized. Little or no aid may result in acute suffering by the families of displaced workers. However, too much aid reduces the incentive for individuals to seek new employment. Compassion must not be allowed to remove economic incentives for self-improvement.

Price provides an answer to the second part of this question. He believes that assistance should take the form of training for new jobs. I strongly disagree with this proposal, since it restricts individual choice. Under the Price plan, a displaced worker must either accept the training offered (perhaps for employment which is unappealing or unsuitable) or get nothing at all. If aid is to be given to displaced workers, I favor making it in the form of cash. The individual worker can then decide how to use the money in his own best interest.

7. *Would an industrial policy of the type proposed by Lee Price straighten out the American economy?*

It is important to recognize that what Lee Price calls an "industrial policy" is actually a form of centralized economic planning. Despite its long and dismal record of failure, there are still many who believe that centralized planning is the only way to achieve economic growth and prosperity. A critical requirement for the success of centralized planning is the ability of the planners to make accurate forecasts of future economic developments. Under the Lee Price plan, a coalition of government experts, industrialists, and labor leaders will decide which industries will grow and which will contract. Given the current state of the art of economic forecasting, it is highly likely that such a coalition will commit serious errors when it makes such choices.[4] Rather than straightening out the American economy, an industrial policy will almost surely make things worse.

8. *Is there an alternative to the industrial policy coupled with trade restrictions proposed by Lee Price?*

Mr. Price and other proponents of an industrial policy are skeptical of the ability of free markets to produce economic advancement. They believe that government, in collaboration with corporate management and organized labor, must plan and direct economic change.

Such skepticism is unfounded. The economic successes of the United States in the past were not due to centralized planning or government-industry-union alliances. Instead, they were produced by private enterprises competing in a profit and loss system.

Competition is the force which drives economic change. Trade restrictions, by reducing competitive pressures, slow the pace of economic progress. If the government really wants to assist major industries in this country, it can do so by reducing regulatory burdens, lowering tax rates, and unilaterally removing all trade barriers. In short, a very attractive alternative to Lee Price's industrial policy with trade restrictions is minimal government involvement in the functioning of the economy with a full commitment to free trade.

NOTES

1. The foreign trade component of Price's blueprint for industrial restructuring is reminiscent of John Stuart Mill's "infant" industries argument. For this reason, it is perhaps appropriate to refer to Price's proposal as the "geriatric" or "senile" industries argument.

2. The dangers of granting "temporary" protection to reorganizing industries are clearly illustrated by the recent experience with import quotas on automobiles.

While some changes were made, American automobile manufacturers pressured the government throughout 1984 to extend the quotas until additional technological improvements were in place. However, if the quotas had not been granted, the American automobile industry would have been forced to become more efficient more rapidly, and it is likely that the required changes could have been made before 1984.

3. Being a rather hard hearted person, I am tempted to ask the question, "Why help the displaced workers at all?" Just as the imposition of import restrictions lessens the incentives for firms to make changes needed to improve efficiency, the granting of aid to individuals lessens their incentive to look for new jobs. However, I concede that there is a consensus in the United States that government must take steps to lessen the costs borne by those who lose their jobs as a result of economic change. Given this consensus, the argument is about how much and what type of aid should be granted.

4. Before adopting an industrial policy which depends upon the ability of central planners to predict the future accurately, it would be advisable to test the foresight of Price's government-business-labor coalition. For example, at the start of each of the next five years, the coalition should be required to announce its predictions of the year's top 20 performing stocks. If the coalition is as collectively omniscient as the success of Lee Price's industrial policy requires, there should be a very high correspondence between its predictions and actual performance. However, in the event the coalition is unable to pick stock market winners consistently, there would be no reason to trust its judgment in making the vital choices of which industries should grow and which should contract.

THE PROGRESSIVITY OF ENDOGENOUS TARIFF POLICY IN GENERAL EQUILIBRIUM

Stephen P. Magee, Leslie Young,

and William A. Brock

INTRODUCTION AND SUMMARY

This paper explores the behavior of lobbies and political parties in their setting of international commercial and industrial policies, particularly tariffs and export subsidies. In our framework, the policies are set by political parties who are power brokers among special interest lobbies and voters. Protectionist and antiprotectionist lobbies channel resources to their favored party to maximize membership income, while the political parties set their policies to maximize their probabilities of election. In such a model, the long-term domestic price of U.S. importables relative to exportables is determined by the tariff supported by the Democrats, the export subsidy supported by the Republicans, and the probabilities of election of the two parties.

This paper investigates the effects of world price and production technology shocks on the domestic political equilibrium and on domestic factor incomes. We find in both cases that the endogenous domestic political sector buffers domestic incomes from external shocks: that is, it acts like a progressive tax. For example, a fall in the price of labor-intensive goods on world markets causes wages to fall by less in the United States with lobbying and politicking than without. The explanation is political-economic arbitrage by the lobbies: the lower wage caused by the reduced price of importables lowers the opportunity cost of lobbying to labor. The labor lobby then transfers labor out of production and into politics. With more labor resources available, the equilibrium tariff is now too low, so that the Democrats raise it. Ironically, after all of the general equilibrium adjustments, the Democrats have a lower probability of election than before. The increased tariff dominates the lowered frequency of Democratic election so that the political adjustments provide a marginal increase in wages which partially offset the original wage drop.

We started this study with the following question: Does special interest lobbying and purely selfish political party behavior reinforce or offset economic advantage? If the former is the case, endogenous politics makes the strong stronger; if the latter, it makes the strong weaker. Our model is so nonaltruistic that Ron Findlay has labeled it the 2-by-4 model, partly because of its blatant emphasis on stark self-interest (and partly because of its 2×2×2×2 structure—2 goods, 2 factors, 2 lobbies, and 2 political parties, all maximizing). Even with this structure, we find here that with both price and technology shocks, the political structure offsets any change in a factor's economic condition: politics is a compensating mechanism. This progressivity result is not the case with all parametric changes. In an earlier paper, Magee and Young (1983) show that endogenous politics reinforces shocks derived from factor endowments and international factor movements. In those cases, the political effects of endowment shocks were regressive.

One implication of our progressivity result with price and technology shocks is that factor incomes will have less long-term variability with endogenous politics than without. However, this is not costless: one or both of the factors have lower incomes because of the lobbying costs.

Do the fortunes of labor and the Democrats move together in such a world? It depends. In the face of world price shocks, what is good for labor is good for the Democrats. In the face of changes in production technologies, what is good for labor is bad for the Democrats. A symmetrical statement applies to the Republicans. All of the results developed from the simulations in this paper use Leontief production functions for the two goods and logit probability of election functions.

Is there empirical support for our progressivity result? We could envision a test in which the labor lobbying for protection would be negatively correlated with the world price of labor-intensive goods. However, this would involve some difficult aggregation problems in product markets and construction of a measure of labor lobbying activity. Baldwin (1976) has constructed a cross-sectional index of the latter using protectionist labor union campaign contributions to congressmen on a specific U.S. trade bill. However, we do not have a time series index of lobbying activity suitable for a direct empirical test. The closest we can come to a measure of protectionist lobbying activity is the number of dumping cases filed in the United States. This was suggested by an interesting study by Takacs (1979). Since this paper contains a long-term model, we would like to abstract from short-term business cycle influences. The latter causes both capital and labor in import-competing industries to lobby for protectionism, while capital and labor in export industries lobby for free trade (see Magee, 1980). Since our dumping data is annual, and hence short-term, we test out political-economic arbitrage hypothesis indirectly. If political and economic markets are effectively arbitraged, we should expect more protectionist pressure in low inflation business cycle troughs and less pressure in high inflation business peaks. We verify this variation on Takacs in the last section of this paper.

The first section of the paper provides a verbal summary of the model. The second section presents the formal model. The third section describes the simulation results of the progressivity outcome for the price and technology shocks. The final section presents the empirical tests.

A DESCRIPTION OF THE MODEL

Voter Behavior

The probability of election model which we use to describe voter behavior was developed earlier by Brock (Brock and Magee, 1974, 1975) and differs from the median voter model in the political science literature. On a single dimension issue such as the one analyzed here (positive vs. negative tariffs), the median voter model predicts that both political parties would choose the same tariff, namely, the one maximizing the welfare of the median voter. However, we chose not to use the median voter approach for four reasons, most of which are related to our understanding of the stylized facts of tariff formation. First, Brock and Magee (1975) showed that neither lobby would contribute resources to either party when the parties quote identical positions. We feel that a theory of special interest politics would be seriously lacking if it did not have lobbies contributing economic resources to the political parties.

Second, it is our impression that special-interest redistributive legislation originates with lobbies rather than voters. For example, milk price supports arise from the milk lobby rather than from a desire from 51 percent of the electorate for a higher income for diary farmers.

Third, by definition, a minority of the electorate favors any given special-interest policy. Further, such issues are relatively unimportant in most campaigns, and so voters are imperfectly informed on them. Assume that only five percent of the electorate benefits from a tariff while another five percent benefits from an export subsidy—these two groups will be on opposite ends of a redistributive spectrum defined by the price of exportables relative to importables. If the other 90 percent of the electorate lose equally from these distortions, the per capita loss can be quite small. Couple this with the insignificance of each voter and we conclude that it pays individual voters to remain uninformed. The median voter model is not very powerful if it is irrational for 90 percent of voters to be uninformed on a redistributive issue such as protection. We speculate that one result of this process is that each party sponsors many redistributive policies and uses the funds to inform voters about all issues of the campaign. Most of the information provided to voters will be from rival parties, who expose the distortionary evils of the policies of the opposing party.

Fourth, most parties are reluctant to reveal their positions on special-interest issues to the electorate. For these reasons, we follow Brock and model the voters as imperfectly informed. We assume that voters choose their parties via a probability of election function which increases in the economic resources held by the party but decreases in the distortionary policy of the party.

The Economy and the Lobbies

It is easiest to remember the details of the model by reference to the United States, after which it was patterned. The model is 2×2×2×2, referring to 2 goods, 2 factors, 2 lobbies, and 2 political parties. Imagine that we divide all U.S. goods into two groups, high tech and low tech: that is, computers (the exportable) and shoes (the importable). The United States has two factors of production: its abundant factor is capital (both physical and human), while its scarce factor is labor (unskilled). Computers use primarily human capital in their production, while shoes use primarily unskilled labor. The United States follows the Heckscher-Ohlin theorem in exporting computers, which use the abundant factor intensively in production, while importing shoes, the labor-intensive good. The Stolper-Samuelson theorem predicts that labor would favor a tariff on shoe imports since this will raise their domestic price, stimulate shoe production, and raise wages, because shoes use a lot of labor in production. Labor forms a lobby which removes labor from productive activity and channels it to one of the parties, perhaps the Democrats, in exchange for a tariff on shoe imports. We ignore the Olson free-rider problem: as a result, our model finds the upper limit on the equilibrium level of lobbying resources by the two lobbies. Similarly, a capital lobby removes capital from production and uses it to help Republicans get elected, in exchange for an export subsidy on computers. Since the world price of computers is fixed, no U.S. producer of computers will sell a computer in the United States at less than what it will receive from exporting, namely, the world price plus the export subsidy. Before an election, the expected domestic product price ratio is the world price adjusted by the equilibrium tariff and the export subsidy, weighted by the probabilities of election of Democrats and Republicans, respectively. Since the economic model is a long-term one and we wish to explain long-term levels of tariffs and export subsidies, we assume that production and consumption decisions are made before political outcomes are revealed. This is equivalent to assuming that production and consumption decisions are based on both the equilibrium tariffs and export subsidies of the two parties weighted by their long-term electoral success ratios.

There is one nagging point, in the perception of special-interest lobbying as a process whereby large, disorganized groups are exploited by small, well-organized ones. We feel that this is the case with both tariff and export subsidy lobbies. On the other hand, in our simple two factor model, one of the factors should have a majority of the electorate and impose its will. One way out of the problem is to construct a three factor model to guarantee that no one factor would have a majority of the voters. However, the modeling costs of such an exercise must outweigh the benefits of the increased realism. Also, after the complications we faced in getting a 2×2×2×2 model to an interested reader, such a model would be difficult to explain. Another way out is to realize that a substantial fraction of the electorate is either uninformed or apathetic, even on redistributive issues. We assume in our model that this fraction is sufficiently large on the issue of protection that neither capital nor labor can control electoral outcomes.

An initially troublesome issue is designing the general equilibrium game structure. Following Magee and Brock (1980) we placed the actors on three tiers: the parties on the top tier; the lobbies on the second tier; and the product markets, factor markets, and voters on the bottom tier. Each actor is a Stackelberg leader vis-à-vis actors directly below them and on lower tiers but acts in Cournot-Nash fashion vis-à-vis actors on the same or higher tiers. Thus, the pro-labor party internalizes the behavior of the labor lobby, the economy, and voters before making their decision on the tariff; the pro-capital party behaves similarly. It turns out that the parties must Stackelberg lead vis-à-vis the lobbies; otherwise, the parties do not set positive distortionary policies in our model and we would have no explanation of tariffs. Consider the Democrats. If the Democrats behaved Cournot-Nash or acted as Stackelberg followers, they would take the level of lobbying contributions from the labor lobby as fixed when they made their tariff decision. In this case, as they raise their tariff above zero, there is no marginal gain in lobbying campaign funds to trade off against the voter disaffection from the tariff. Thus, these two game theoretic formulations imply that parties would never set positive redistributive policies, and for this reason, we rule them out.

How is the equilibrium tariff set? When the Democrats set their tariff, they trade off the favorable effect of the tariff on campaign contributions from the labor lobby against the direct loss of votes caused by voters disaffected by the tariff. At the Democrats' equilibrium tariff, the marginal gain in the votes which they obtained from the additional campaign contributions from the labor lobby will just be offset by the marginal loss of votes because of the distortionary tariff. At any lower tariff than this, the former effect will be larger than the latter and the Democrats would gain votes by raising their tariff. For development of parties maximizing their probabilities of election with special interest lobbies or the "vote maximization model" see Brock and Magee (1974, 1975), and Peltzman (1976).

While the Democrats set a tariff and the Republicans set an export subsidy, there is really only a single redistributive issue in the model: an export subsidy is equivalent to a negative tariff. Since only relative product prices matter in a two goods model, the two parties are essentially battling over high versus low relative product prices. However, we do not end up with an Hotelling equilibrium with the two parties selecting identical positions on the relative price line: the probabilities of election are two dimensional (resources and policy positions) and identical policy positions cannot be a full equilibrium, because the lobbies would not contribute to either party.

Consider now the behavior of the lobbies. Let the labor lobby remove one worker from productive activity and transfer his services to assisting the Democrats in their political competition. All labor gains because the Democrats sponsor a positive tariff which raises the price of labor-intensive goods, which raises wages. Since the lobby is a Stackelberg follower, it takes the tariff as given. However, the lobby leads vis-à-vis both voters and the economy. Thus, the marginal gain to the labor lobby from contributing to the Democrats is calculated by figuring how much the increase in the probability of Democratic election increases the expected domestic relative product price of the low-tech good and then calculating the Stolper-Samuelson effect of this product price change on wages. Notice that this wage change must be multiplied by all of the labor still productively employed, since they all share in it. If this change in the wage bill of all productive labor exceeds the value of the single laborer placed into political activity, the decision to lobby was a rational one. The removal of labor from productive activity will proceed until the marginal gains and marginal costs balance; this point defines the lobbying equilibrium. The location of this margin is obviously affected by the success of the lobby in overcoming its Olsonian (1965) free rider problem. Since the parties Stackelberg lead, the lobbies take the party positions as given. For this reason, they follow the "campaign contribution specialization theorem" and contribute only to the most favored party (see Brock and Magee, 1975). The lobby does this because its only marginal effects on the political system are through the probabilities of election, which are constant and sum to one. If the labor lobby contribution raises the Democrats' chances from 30 to 35 percent, it would obviously be foolish for them to give also to the Republicans, since this would help the negative tariff party and lower the Democrats' chances below 35 percent. Magee and Brock (1976) have generalized the theorem and shown that in an n-party system, a lobby should give to, at most, $n - 1$ parties.

To summarize, all actors display explicit maximizing behavior, including free riding voters who rely on rival parties rather than their own investments in information. The voter's choice of his favored party is also rational, in that he has a higher probability of voting for parties with lower distortions and more resources. In our model, goods markets and factor markets are perfectly competitive; the economy is small enough so that world product prices can be given as exogenous; product markets take the political outcomes and the policies as given; thus, domestic product prices are set by a combination of world prices and domestic political considerations. As an aside, it is a wonder that econometric models do as well as they do in explaining domestic relative product prices, given the political complications that we observe in their establishment. Each of the lobbies makes a decision to remove part of its factor from economic activity and place it into lobbying in a way which maximizes the welfare of that factor. Each of the political parties sets its redistributive policy in a way which maximizes its probability of election.

THE MODEL

The economic model is the simple 2×2 case (see Young and Magee, 1982). There are two goods, each produced using two factors, capital and labor. As usual, we assume that the production functions exhibit constant returns to scale, and no factor intensity reversals. The numerator is good 1, the more capital-intensive good. Let P^d be the domestic price of good 2 and let W and R be the wage and rental rates. We assume that P^d does not induce specialization in production so that factor rewards depend only on P^d and are independent of factor endowments (ignoring politics). Since increases in P^d help labor and hurt capital, the owners of each factor form a lobby to influence P^d.

The country is small and faces a fixed international price P for good 2, which is imported. There are two political parties: "Republicans" and "Democrats," which use their policies to bid for votes and for political contributions. The Republican policy is to set a domestic price of PS, for example, by subsidizing exports of good 1 by a factor $1/S$. The Democratic policy is to set the domestic price at PT, for example, by an ad valorem tariff $T-1$ on imports. State PS occurs with probability π and PT with probability $(1-\pi)$. Political outcomes are random and are made frequently relative to economic decisions, so that the economy (production and consumption) operates at an expectational equilibrium in relative prices. Since π is the probability of Republican success (with voters, the judiciary, the legislature and the bureaucracy), the domestic price used by producers and consumers in the economy is:

$$P^d = \pi PS + (1 - \pi)PT \tag{1}$$

Let the probability of Republican success, π, depend on (a) the resources each party has for electioneering, (b) the policies adopted by the two parties. Regarding (a), we shall assume that each party's probability of election increases with the resources that it receives from the lobbies. Since Equation (1) implies that workers benefit from increases in P^d, the worker lobby contributes resources only to the party espousing the higher P^d, following Magee and Brock's (1976) campaign contribution specialization theorem. The capital lobby contributes only to Republicans, since they earn a negative expected return from contributing to Democrats. Regarding (b), we shall assume that each party suffers a reduced probability of election as its policy departs further from free trade, for fixed values of the other variables. The rationale for this general voter effect is that voters have some perception of the economic benefits of free trade; they may also resent policies benefiting special-interest groups at the expense of the general welfare. We suppose that each *lobby* chooses its political contributions in order to maximize the net regard of the factor that it represents, while each party chooses its policy in order to maximize its probability of election. Many combinations of Nash and Stackelberg behavior are possible amongst the four players in this political game. As noted earlier, we assume that each party leads its own lobby in a Stackelberg fashion, but adopts Nash behavior toward all the other players, while each lobby adopts Nash behavior toward all other players.

The following provides an overview of the calculations made by the four major actors:

1. By contributing capital to the Republicans, capitalists can increase the probability of a high domestic relative price for

good 1. This increases their expected rental rate via the Stolper-Samuelson effect. However, increased political contributions mean that this higher rental rate is earned by fewer units of productive capital.

2. Similarly, workers must trade off the higher expected wage rate from political contributions to Democrats against the reduction in the units of productive labor earning this higher rate.
3. Republicans can enter the political "market" by announcing a policy of subsidizing exports of good 1. They calculate in a Stackelberg fashion that an increased subsidy rate will "purchase" more political contributions by capital which can be used to increase their probability of election. The cost is the increased voter hostility excited by their interventionist policy.
4. Similar remarks apply mutatis mutandis to the Democrats.

In the special case with a Leontief production technology and a logit probability of election function, it is possible to solve explicitly for optimal lobby and party behavior (for details, see Young and Magee, 1982). We measure capital and labor so that one unit of good 1 requires one unit of capital and one unit of labor. We measure good 2 so that one unit requires one unit of labor. Let A be the units of capital required to produce a unit of good 2. These conventions simplify our formula and entail no loss of generality within the input/output model. We assume that $A < 1$, so that good 2 is indeed relatively labor intensive. Let the total endowments of capital and labor be κ_0 and λ_0 and let their political contributions be κ and λ. We shall confine attention to equilibria in which both factors are fully employed and both goods are produced, that is, where:

$$A < (\kappa_0 - \kappa)/(\lambda_o - \lambda) < 1 \qquad (2)$$

and:

$$A < P^d < 1 \qquad (3)$$

If profit maximization leads to a finite demand for both factors, then, recalling that good 1 is the numerator:

$$W + R = 1$$

$$W + AR = P^d$$

Therefore, the equilibrium wage and rental rates are:

$$R = \frac{1 - P^d}{1 - A} \qquad W = \frac{P^d - A}{1 - A} \tag{4}$$

Notice that $\partial R/\partial P^d < 0$, and $\partial W/\partial P^d > 0$, as implied by the Stolper-Samuelson Theorem.

In the political sector, we suppose that the function $\pi(\kappa, \lambda, S, T)$ giving the probability of Republican victory has the logit form, which is widely used to model dichotomous choices (e.g., Theil, 1970). Under the most general logit models, the odds, $\pi/(1-\pi)$, of a Republican victory would be a loglinear function of the explanatory variables. However, we choose the following specialized form (see Young and Magee, 1985):

$$\pi(\kappa, \lambda, S, T,) = 1/[1 + (L_1 + \lambda)/(K_1 + \kappa)ST] \tag{5}$$

This function has a number of desirable properties:

$$0 \leq \pi \leq 1, \quad \pi_\lambda < 0, \quad \pi_{\lambda\lambda} > 0, \quad \pi_\kappa > 0, \quad \pi_{\kappa\kappa} < 0, \pi_{\kappa\lambda} < 0$$

$$\pi_S > 0, \quad \pi_{SS} < 0, \quad \pi_T > 0, \pi_{TT} < 0, \quad \pi_{ST} < 0$$

(A subscript denotes partial differentiation with respect to the corresponding variable). The variables κ and λ are the desired levels of contributions by the capital and labor lobbies, respectively: The parameters K_1 and L_1 are constants and will play an important role in determining the equilibrium of the political system. In Equation (5), a higher value of K_1 implies that, for any κ, a given change in λ will have a smaller effect on π. Thus, K_1 measures the intrinsic resistance of the political system to political contributions by the labor lobby. Similar methods apply to L_1. Increases in the parameter measuring the system's resistance to one lobby's contributions have effects similar to increases in the political contribution of the other lobby. Therefore, to simplify our formula, we carry out the analysis in terms of the "effective" renter and worker political contributions:

$$K \equiv K_1 + \kappa, L \equiv L_1 + \lambda \tag{6}$$

With these definitions Equation (6) becomes:

$$\pi = 1/(1 + L/KST) = KST/(KST + L) \tag{7}$$

We recast the choices of the two lobbies in terms of K and L. Let the total endowments of effective capital and labor be:

$$K_0 \equiv \kappa_0 + K_1, \quad L_o \equiv \lambda_o + L_1 \tag{8}$$

Then the quantities of capital and labor used in production are:

$$\kappa_0 - \kappa = K_o - \mathrm{K}, \quad \lambda_0 - \lambda = L_0 - L \tag{9}$$

By Equation (4), the expected rates of factor reward are:

$$\bar{R} \equiv \{\pi(1 - \mathrm{PS}) + (1 - \pi)(1 - PT)\}/(1 - A) \tag{10}$$

$$\bar{W} \equiv \{\pi(PS - A) + (1 - \pi)(PT - A)\}/(1 - A) \tag{11}$$

The rentier lobby maximizes its expected return on productive capital, $(K_o - K)\bar{R}$. By Equations (9), (10), and (7) it solves:

$$\max_{K_1 \leq K \leq K_0}$$

$$e(K) \equiv (K_0 - K)\{KST(1-PS) + L(1-PT)\}/(KST+L)(1-A) \tag{12}$$

The worker lobby maximizes its expected return on productive labor, $(L_0 - L_1)\bar{W}$. By Equations (9), (11), and (7) it solves:

$$\max_{L_1 \leq L \leq L_0} f(L) \equiv (L_0 - L)\{KST(PS-A) + L(PT-A)\}/(KST+L)(1-A) \qquad (13)$$

The strategies of the parties are:

$$\text{Republicans} \qquad \max_{S} \quad \pi \qquad (14)$$

$$\text{Democrats} \qquad \min_{T} \quad \pi \qquad (15)$$

THE SIMULATIONS

This section uses solutions to the model developed in the second section. We examine economic and political equilibria satisfying the equations in the second section for all possible "countries" conforming to the following stylized facts: both goods are produced; factor incomes are positive; both lobbies participate and contribute to the political process; and both parties sponsor a distortionary policy (i.e., Democrats sponsor a positive tariff and Republicans sponsor a positive export subsidy). All countries fitting this description would have (1) the relative production technology parameter $A < 1$; (2) the world price in the interval $A < P < 1$; and (3) the free trade endowment in the interval $A < (K_0 - K_1)/(L_0 - L_1) < 1$; and (4) the elasticity of electoral outcomes with respect to political contributions would be high (we set $K_1 = L_1 = 1$ and $L_0 = 1$ throughout). We performed a grid search over the logically possible parameter values and found 61 economies conforming to the conditions above. The only parameters to differ from "economy to economy" are factor endowments, product prices on world markets, and the relative factor intensities of production (i.e., $(K_0 - K)$ $(L_0 - L_1)$, P and A). We compare the incomes of capital and labor in the full political-economic equilibrium (with lobbying and policy distortions) with their incomes under free trade (no lobbying and no distortions) across these economies.

We first divided the economies into three groups. The first group contains those in which capital gained the most from the political system. This we defined to be any economy in which capital's income with endogenous politics exceeded its income with free trade. There were ten such "capital dominant" economies. Group three contained 27 "labor dominant" economies, in which total labor income, even after lobbying exceeded labor income with free trade. That left 24 economies in which both capital and labor were worse off with lobbying, tariffs, and export subsidies than they would have been under free trade. The latter led us to formulate a prisoners' dilemma explanation of the puzzle of tariffs (Young and Magee, 1985). Our view was that tariffs and redistributive policies generally can emerge as equilibrium outcomes, even when they make everyone in an economy worse off if the payoffs to the lobbies conform to those in a prisoners' dilemma.

In this paper, we are interested in explaining why certain economies ended up in groups 1 and 3; that is, some factors get a lot while others got only a little out of the political system. Initially, we were surprised to find that the factors which got the most out of the political system (capital in group 1 countries and labor in group 3 countries) were those with the lowest incomes initially. That is, the initial free trade rental/wage ratio was lowest for the capital dominant group 1 (.75); next lowest for group 2 (1.11), and highest for the labor dominant group 3 (2.58). This suggested a compensation mechanism or a progressivity effect at work.

There are only three parameters, A, P and $(K_0 - K)/(L_0 - L)$, varying from economy to economy, so our next job was to consider which were responsible for the result. We knew from Magee and Young (1985) that increases in a country's capital endowment led to increasing capital returns: that is, when a country had higher returns to capital (net of all lobbying costs) than existed on world markets, capital would enter, further strengthening the local procapital party, and so forth, causing endogenous politics continuously to reinforce economic strength. The capital endowment effect is clearly regressive. Thus, our results must be due to differences among the economies in the technology and world price parameters, A and P. We know that low free trade

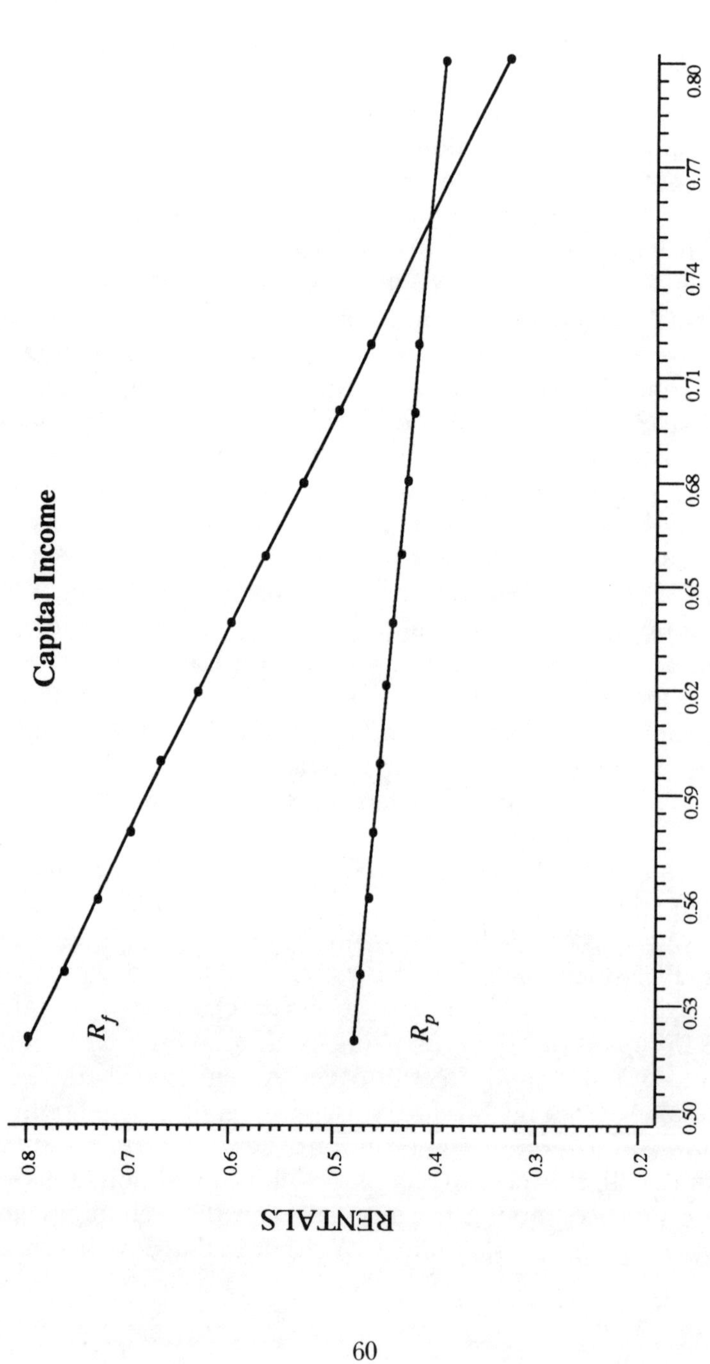
Capital Income
RENTALS
P
R_f
R_p
0.8
0.7
0.6
0.5
0.4
0.3
0.2
0.50
0.53
0.56
0.59
0.62
0.65
0.68
0.71
0.74
0.77
0.80

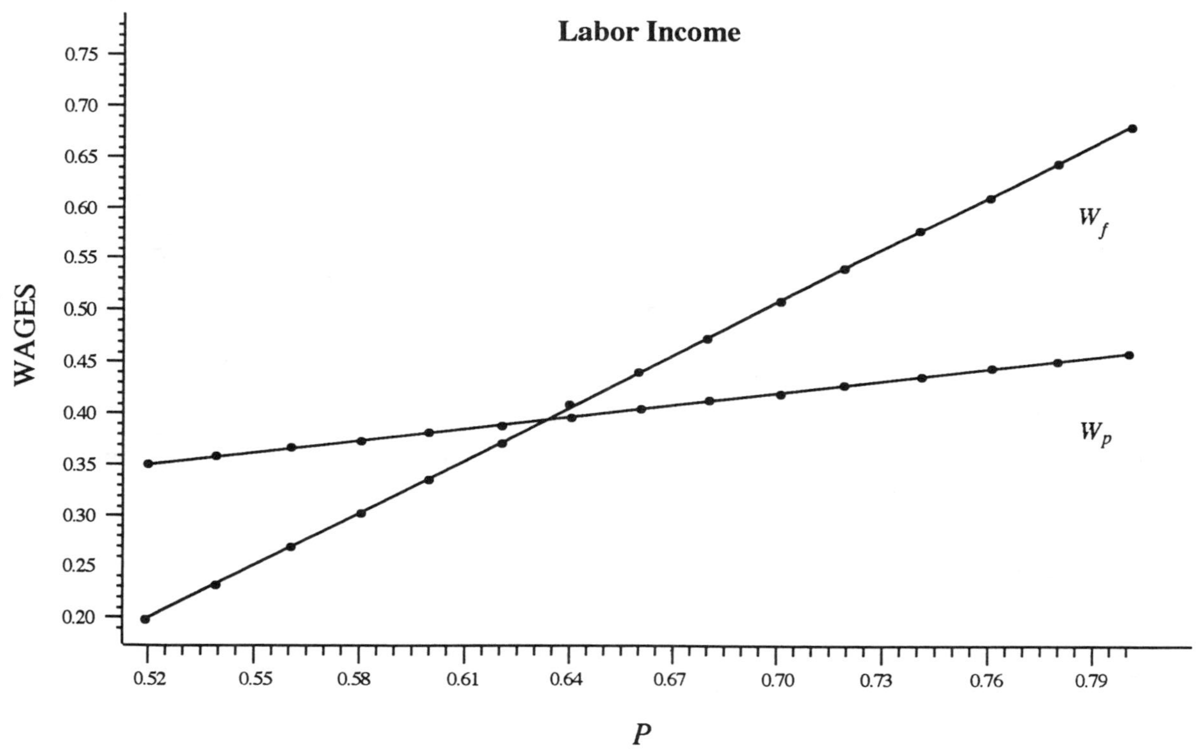

Figure 1. Factor Incomes Related to World Product Prices

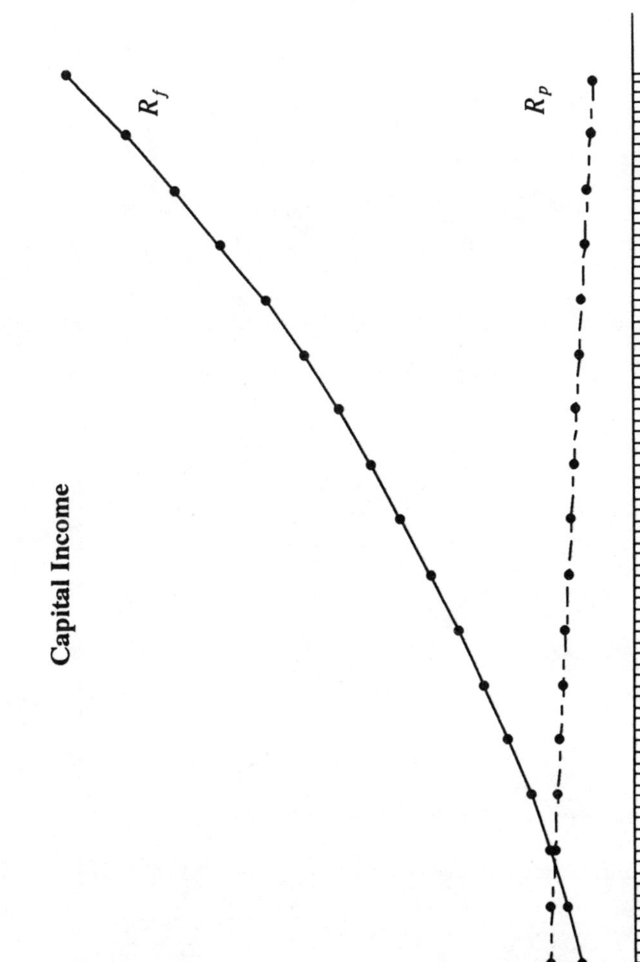
Capital Income
RENTALS
R
R_f
R_p
0.80
0.75
0.70
0.65
0.60
0.55
0.50
0.45
0.40
0.28
0.32
0.36
0.40
0.44
0.48
0.52
0.56
0.60

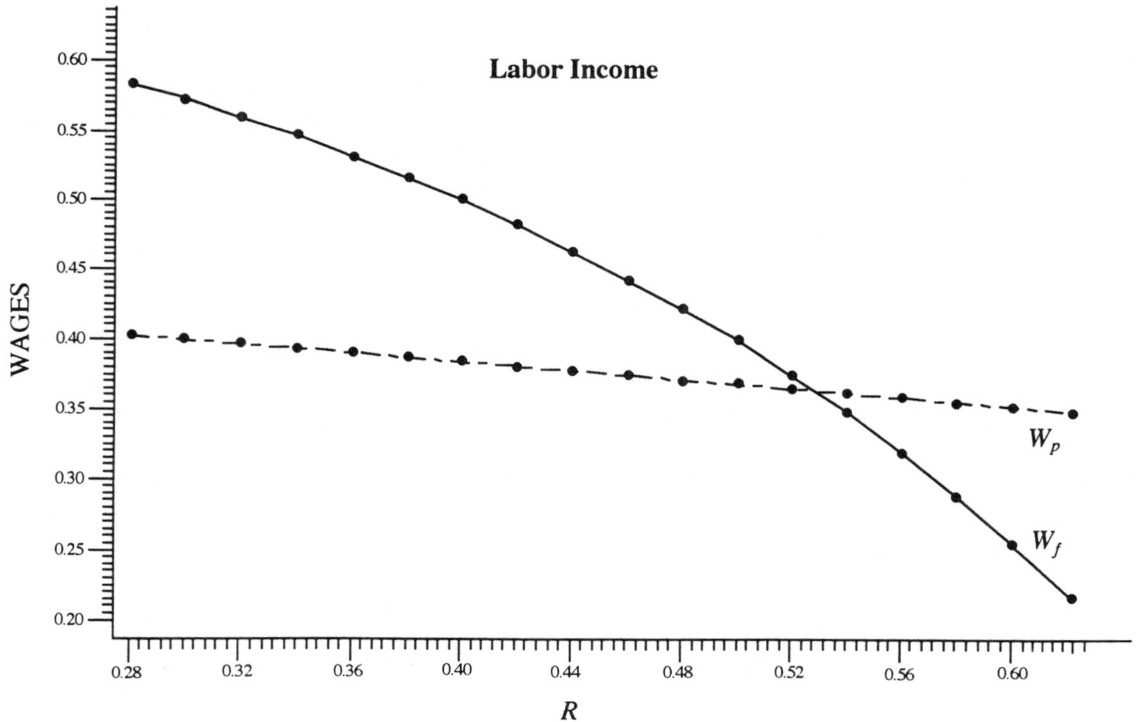

Figure 2. Factor Incomes Related to Production Technology
($p = .70$)

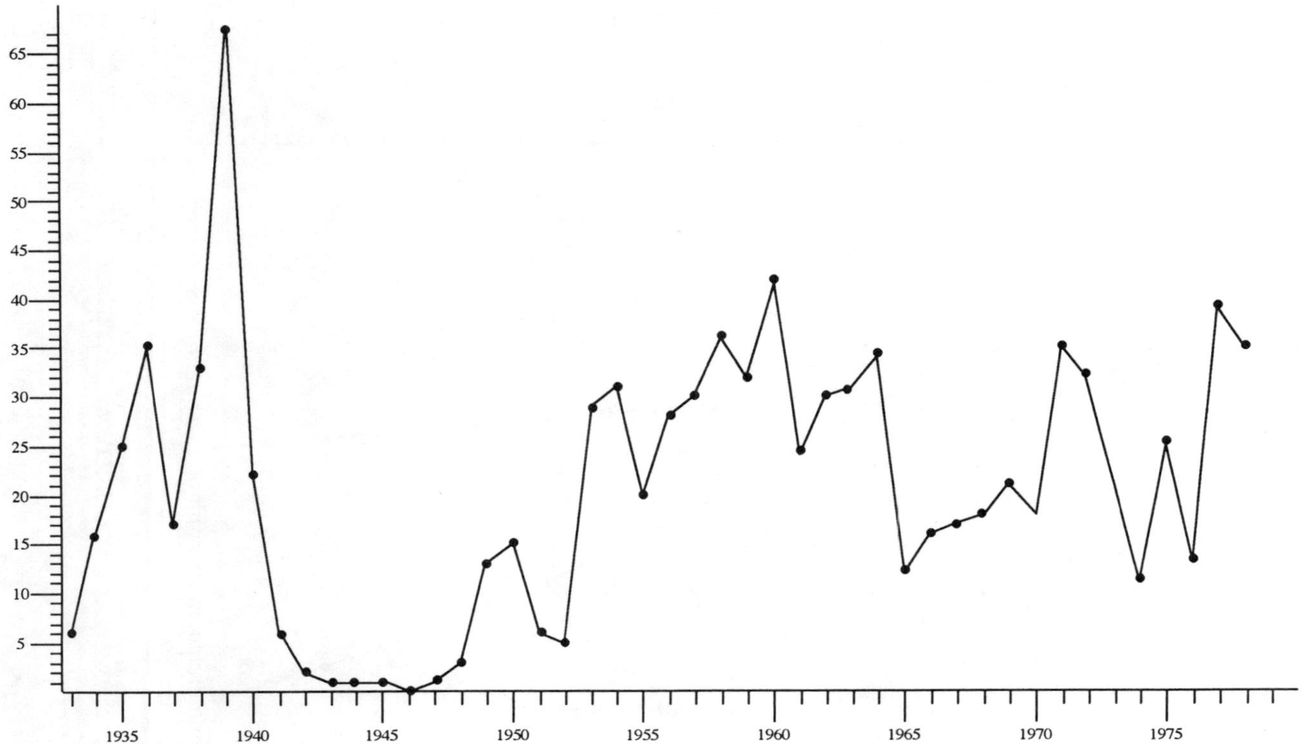

Figure 3. Index of Protectionist Pressure in the United States, 1933-1978: Number of Dumping Cases Filed

rentals in the group 1 countries are associated with high world prices of the labor intensive good (P) and/or low capital/output ratios for good 2 (A). Comparative statics in all 61 economies revealed that the ratio of capital income in the general economic-political equilibrium to capital income with free trade always increased with greater economic disadvantage: that is, with higher P and lower A. These simulation outcomes are the basis of our compensation/progressivity effect. Obviously, our results are related to the functional forms we have chosen. At this stage, we do not know their sensitivity to the choice of production and voting functions.

Figures 1 and 2 are representative of the response of factor incomes to change in prices and technology. In both figures, we defined $R_p = (K_o - K)\bar{R}/K_0$ and $W_p = (L_0 - L)\bar{W}/L_0$ [see above for a discussion of Equations (12) and (13)]. These rentals and wages are thus after lobbying expenses have been removed. In Figure 1, we vary P, holding A constant at .40 and K_0/L_0 constant at 71/101. As indicated earlier, $K_1 = L_1 = 1$. Notice that Figure 1 illustrates the progressivity effects of the endogenous political equilibria in response to price shocks. Notice in Figure 3 that a rise in the world price of the labor intensive good does raise wages and lower rentals. However, the political sector weakens the economic effects. In fact, the simulations show that elasticities of R_p and W_p with respect to P are always less than one in absolute value. Thus, in contrast to the usual Stolper-Samuelson conclusion, the improvement in the returns to labor could be offset by the increase in the cost of living if labor's tastes are sufficiently biased toward good 2. Notice also that for the parameter values chosen, a world price of good 2 below .62 causes labor to earn more than it would have with free trade while a price above .76 causes capital to get more than under free trade. For world prices between .62 and .76, both factors are worse off with lobbying and politics than they would have been with free trade (these are prisoners' dilemma cases). Figure 2 reports similar results for changes in A. The parameters chosen for Figure 2 are $P = .70$; $K_o = 91$; $L_0 = 100$; $K_1 = 1$; and $L_1 = 1$.

AN INDIRECT EMPIRICAL TEST

Is it possible to test the progressivity result? Empirically, we would expect to see U.S. labor seek protection whenever world prices of labor-intensive goods fall. This sounds easy but it is fraught with difficult aggregation and factor intensity issues. It would be easier to test the proposition that factors substitute toward protectionist lobbying activity in periods of slack markets, and reduce their protectionist pressure in periods of tight markets, that is, a test of the more general proposition of political-economic arbitrage. When the rate of return on economic activity falls, we expect rational lobbies to transfer resources into political activity.

Our test of political-economic arbitrage is a simple one. We examine whether an index of protectionist pressure (the number of dumping cases filed with the U.S. Treasury) covaries positively or negatively with the U.S. business cycle. When U.S. labor markets and product markets are slack, we expect U.S. firms and labor to exert greater pressures for protectionism, since the opportunity cost of political activity is lower. Our measure of the tightness of U.S. product and factor markets is the U.S. unemployment rate. In addition, we know that protectionist appeals will be tempered by rational expectations about their changes of success. When the U.S. inflation rate is high, consumer pressures mount for import liberalization and the political system is less receptive to protectionist arguments. Protectionists should anticipate this and make fewer protectionist demands in high inflation periods. Thus, our second determinant of U.S. protectionist pressure is the U.S. inflation rate.

When we regress the U.S. protectionist index on U.S. unemployment and U.S. inflation, both variables are significant over the period 1933-1978. The index of protectionist pressure is shown in Figure 3 and the estimated equation is shown in Table 1. Over this 45-year period, the estimates show that the elasticity of protectionist pressure with respect to the rate of unemployment is .9. Thus a 10 percent increase in the rate of unemployment (e.g., from 5 percent to 5.5 percent) is associated with a 9 percent rise in protectionist pressure. The equation indicates that each percentage point increase in the inflation rate of the U.S. wholesale

Table 1. Equation Explaining U.S. Protectionism, Estimated from Annual Data, 1933-1977 (t-Values in Parentheses)

$$\log P = -.15 - 1.38\,DUM + .92 \log U - 5.67\,(\Delta WPI/WIP)$$
$$\quad\;\; (.26)\;\; (-7.54) \qquad (6.77) \qquad (-3.88)$$

$R^2 = .72$ standard error of estimation = .58

Average Value	*Variable*	*Definition*
26.7	P	index of protectionist pressure in the United States (number of dumping cases filed with the U.S. Treasury)
.44	DUM	dummy variable (equals 1.0 for 1933 through 1952 and0 for 1953 through 1977)
7.3	U	U.S. unemployment rate in percent
.041	$\Delta WPI/WPI$	inflation rate in the U.S. wholesale price index expressed as a proportion (i.e., .06 for 6 percent inflation)

index (e.g., from .06 to .07) lowers protectionist demands by 5.7 percent.

We view these results as an indirect corroboration of the assumption of political-economic arbitrage needed for our progressivity result. The results are not new in the literature on the counter cyclicality of protectionist pressure. For example, Takacs (1981) has shown that escape clause cases are counter cyclical. She used more explanatory variables than we, although a shorter estimation period (1949-1979). She also reported that her model was less successful in explaining antidumping cases than escape clause cases. Nor did she include the inflation rate as an explanatory variable.

As an aside, the equation reported in Table 1 suggests that a locus of constant protectionist pressure can be drawn which is positively sloped in an inflation rate-unemployment rate diagram (see Figure 4). This curve defines the long-term political-economic arbitrage equilibrium which held for the entire estimation period. (We have drawn the now ancient Phillips curve in the same figure for reference.) Points to the left of our curve of constant protectionist pressure are associated with business cycle peaks in

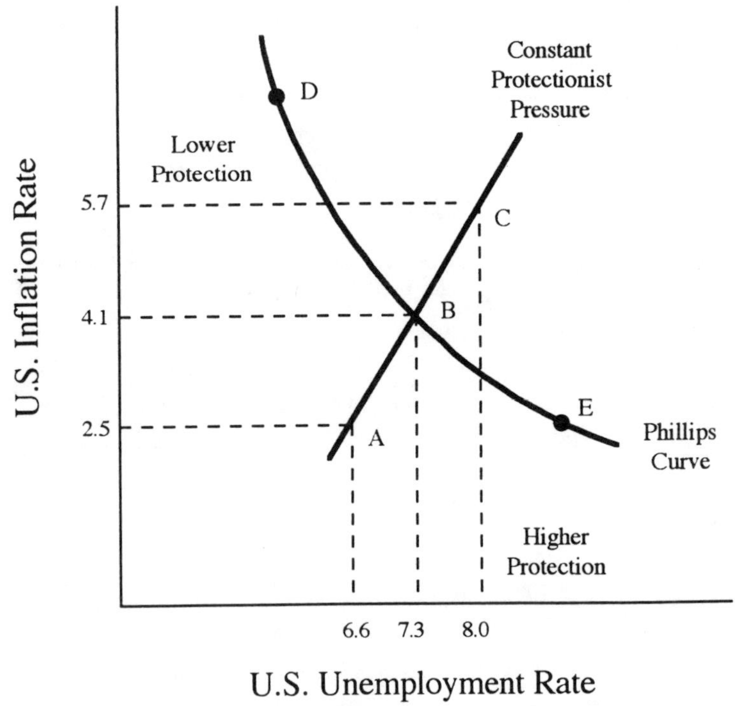

Figure 4.

which the lobbies were exerting less protectionist pressure than the historical average. Points to the right of the curve are associated with troughs and heavier protectionist pressure. In terms of the language of our model in Section 2, the lobbying ratios for protectionists relative to antiprotectionists are low to the left of the curve and high to the right. Movements toward or away from the curve are associated with political-economic arbitrage disequilibria in which the lobbies will be changing their composition of political and economic activity.

Are there other uses of the inflation-unemployment model of protectionism? The addition of the inflation rate to these models provides a link with macroeconomic discussions of protectionism. It also generates insights into changes in protectionist pressure in the 1970s. Notice in Figure 3 that protectionist pressure rose considerably from 1973-74 to 1976-77. The standard explanation was the softening of U.S. economic activity reflected in the rise in the U.S. unemployment rate from 5.3 percent to 7.4 percent. However, our model indicates that most of the increase in protectionism over this period was due to the decrease in the inflation rate (from 16 percent to 5.3 percent) rather than the increase in the unemployment rate. (Our model is off in that it overpredicts the increase in protectionism; however, the point here is the allocation of explained change between unemployment and inflation).

The Congress overwhelmingly passed the nonprotectionist Trade Bill of 1979. This is not inconsistent with our model's prediction of a 27 percent decline in protectionist pressure from the first five months of 1977 to the first five months of 1979. This decrease is explained by the drop in the U.S. unemployment rate from 7.3 to 5.8 and the rise in the U.S. inflation rate from 9.4 percent to 10.8 percent during this period.

REFERENCES

Baldwin, Robert. 1979. "The Political Economy of U.S. Trade Policy," *The Bulletin.* Center for Study of Financial Institutions, Graduate School of Business Administration, New York University. Bulletin 1976(4).

Baldwin, Robert. 1982. "The Political Economy of Protectionism." In *Import Competition and Response,* ed. by J.N. Bhagwati, 263-286. Chicago: University of Chicago Press.

Bhagwati, Jagdish. 1980. "Lobbying and Welfare." *Journal of Public Economics* 14 (December): 355-363.

Bhagwati, Jagdish. 1982. "Directly Unproductive, Profit-Seeking (DUP) Activities." *Journal of Political Economy* 90 (December): 988-1002.

Bhagwati, Jagdish and T.N. Srinivasan. 1980. "Revenue Seeking: A Generalization of the Theory of Tariffs." *Journal of Political Economy.* 88 (December): 1069-1087.

Brock, William A. and Stephen P. Magee. 1975. "The Economics of Pork-Barrel Politics." *Report 7511,* Center for Mathematical Studies in Business and Economics. University of Chicago, February.

Brock, William A. and Stephen P. Magee. 1980. "Tariff Formation in a Democracy." In *Current Issues in Commercial Policy and Diplomacy,* ed. by John Black and Brian Hindley, 1-9. New York: St. Martin's Press.

Feenstra, Robert C. and Jagdish N. Bhagwati. 1982. "Tariff Seeking and the Efficient Tariff." In *Import Competition and Response,* ed. by Jagdish N. Bhagwati, 145-258. Chicago: University of Chicago Press.

Findlay, Ronald and Stanislaw Wellisz. 1982. "Endogenous Tariffs, the Political Economy of Trade Restrictions, and Welfare." In *Import Competition and Response,* ed. by Jagdish Bhagwati, 223-234. Chicago: University of Chicago Press.

Frey, Bruno S. and Friedrich Schneider. 1982. "International Political Economy: An Emerging Field." *Seminar Paper No. 227,* Institute for International Economic Studies, University of Stockholm, November.

Harberger, Arnold C. 1962. "The Incidence of the Corporation Income Tax," *Journal of Political Economy* 70 (June): 215-240.

Jones, Ronald. 1971. "A Three-Factor Model in Theory, Trade and History." In *Trade, Balance of Payments and Growth: Papers in International Economics in Honor of Charles P. Kindleberger,* ed. Jagdish N. Bhagwati et al., 3-21. Amsterdam: North Holland Press.

Krueger, Anne O. 1974. "The Political Economy of the Rent-Seeking Society," *American Economic Review* 64 (June): 291-303.

Magee, Stephen P., and William A. Brock. 1976. "The Campaign Contribution Specialization Theorem." Mimeo, University of Texas at Austin, February.

Magee, Stephen P. and William A. Brock. 1983. "A Model of Politics, Tariffs and Rent Seeking in General Equilibrium." In *Human Resources, Employment and Development. Volume 3: The Problems of Developed Countries,* ed. B. Weisbrod and H. Huhes, 497-523. London: MacMillan.

Magee, Stephen P., William A. Brock, and Leslie Young. 1989. *Black Hole Tariffs and Endogeneous Policy Theory.* New York: Cambridge University Press.

Mayer, Wolfgang. 1984. "Endogenous Tariff Formation." *American Economic Review* 74 (December).

Messerlin, Patrick A. 1981. "The Political Economy of Protectionism: The Bureaucratic Case." *Weltwirtschaftliches Archiv* 117 (3): 469-495.

Olson, Mancur. 1965. *The Logic of Collective Action.* Cambridge, MA: Harvard University Press.

Otani, Wyoshihiko. 1980. "Strategic Equilibrium of Tariffs in General Equilibrium." *Econometrica* 48 (April): 643-662.

Tollison, Robert D. 1982. "Rent Seeking: A Survey." *Kyklos* 35: 28-47.

Tullock, Gordon. 1967. "The Welfare Costs of Tariffs, Monopolies, and Theft." *Western Economic Journal* 5 (June): 224-232.

Young, Leslie. 1982. "Comment on Findlay and Wellisz." In *Import Competition and Response,* ed. Jagdish Bhagwati, 238-243. Chicago: University of Chicago Press.

Young, Leslie, and Stephen P. Magee. 1982. "A Prisoner's Dilemma Theory of Endogenous Tariffs." University of Texas at Austin, April.

Young, Leslie, and Stephen P. Magee. 1986. "Endogenous Protection, Factor Returns and Resource Allocation." *Review of Economic Studies* 53:407-419.

COMMENT ON "THE PROGRESSIVITY OF ENDOGENOUS TARIFF POLICY IN GENERAL EQUILIBRIUM"

Tim S. Campbell

I found the paper by Magee, Young, and Brock to be both interesting and informative. This paper apparently represents an extension of a substantial amount of earlier work on their part concerning the economics of politics. I must confess that, prior to reading their paper, I was largely ignorant of this literature. My comments undoubtedly will reflect this ignorance. I have very few comments to make on the specific results and simulation presented in the paper. The results seem reasonable and interesting, and it even seems plausible that they could have predictive power, if the practical obstacles facing empirical testing discussed by the authors can be overcome. My comments on their paper are really directed more toward evaluating the reasonableness of the framework they are using than the specific analysis presented in this paper. The answer to almost all of these questions raised here may simply be that it is hard to take these things into account in a "2 × 4" model. If that is the stumbling block, then I would encourage the authors to move on to the "N × M" model as rapidly as possible.

The basic format of their paper is as follows. The voting population is divided into three groups. One group is labor and another capital, while the third is alligned with neither factor of production. The first two groups combined represent a relatively small proportion of the total voting population. Labor and capital favor subsidies for their respective groups and attempt to use the political process to obtain these subsidies. The third and largest group favors "free trade." This means they understand that subsidies are not in their interests. However, and this is crucial, they are subject to some kind of "persuasion" (my word rather than theirs) from an entity known as a political party. Indeed, it appears that the purpose of the political party is to sell persuasion. Presumably, the reason the third group is subject to persuasion, while the first two are not, is that the per unit cost of a subsidy to either of the other groups is small, since they are large in number. Hence, the free trade group has a lower incentive to become well informed. Relative ignorance then creates an opportunity for persuasion. Persuasion is purchased through cash contributions by capital or labor lobbies to political parties. The political parties then spend these cash contributions to influence the chance they will be elected. The probability of a given party being elected increases with the amount it spends on persuasion while it decreases with the amount of the subsidy it says it will provide to the interest group it supports.

My principal comment has to do with the property rights of political parties, or sellers of persuasion. In the proposed model political parties are inherently alligned with interest groups. The two minority interests appear to have ownership rights to parties with given technology for persuasion. But the majority free trade group has no such political party. It is as if the last group had ownership rights to a party or firm with such poor persuasion technology that it was not viable to use it. What would happen if all groups had equal access to persuasion technology? Put another way, what would happen if the large free trade group could form a political party which was in favor of free trade? Presumably, unless the parties which are implicitly owned by the minority interests have extraordinarily effective persuasion technology, they will always lose an election. In fact, it is not really clear what persuasion actually is in such a world. I imagine one would have to assume that it may not be obvious to any voter group whether a given policy entails a subsidy or not. Then, persuasion would involve convincing the voting public that a given policy really has no subsidy and therefore deserves the votes of the free trade group, when in fact it does contain a subsidy. Whoever would appear to have the comparative advantage in such persuasion would appear to be the dominant party.

This line of reasoning also causes one to question the necessary link between parties and interest groups. Suppose the persuasion technology is not owned by a given interest group. Casual empiricism would suggest this is the more reasonable assumption. Now interest groups would compete for the services of firms with persuasion technology. It seems reasonable to expect that the free trade group would be at a disadvantage in this competition, since gains and losses from efficient persuasion per capita are small for this group relative to the small special interest groups. At least this would seem to be the case in a single period world.

However, if ownership of persuasive technology is separate from interest groups, and if voters can learn about the accuracy of persuasion over time, then a multiperiod model might produce interesting new twists. The key is that, if learning is possible, then a comparative advantage in persuasion technology will be dissipated over time with use. That is, people who attempt to persuade the free trade group that a given policy is really in their interests will be found out as the true effects of the policy become known. Unless their technological advantage extends to the realm of ex post facto explanations or excuses for the actual effects of their policies, they are not likely to be believed again. The durability of the persuasion technology will surely affect its price. But the more important question, from the vantage point of the present paper, is whether a specific persuasive effort is identified with an interest group. That is, does the interest group itself lose credibility when the true effect of policies are discovered?

Once you create a separation between the interest group and the party, it then seems fair to ask whether or not the party, once elected, is committed to the interests of the minority group which may have initially funded it. If their interests are separate, it would appear to be optimal for any party to change to the interests of the free traders once elected. Obviously, if learning were highly imperfect, or persuasion could be continued indefinitely, the incentive to switch would be limited.

I raise these points, first because they seem to me to be interesting issues about the general model used by Magee, Young, and Brock; but also because I am not convinced that their specific conclusion will hold up in a more general model of the political process. The problem is that since their results come from a simulation of their political model, it is simply difficult to tell what might happen if a new political model is used. I don't perceive this to be a particularly negative comment about their work. This is simply an inherent difficulty in a simulation based analysis.

On the whole, I think the line of research the authors are pursuing is interesting and important. However, it may be hard to get definitive results without using highly arbitrary models of the political process.

ECONOMIC DETERMINANTS OF U.S. TRADE POLICY:
AN EMPIRICAL ANALYSIS

Victor A. Canto and J. Kimball Dietrich

INTRODUCTION

Record trade deficits, inflation rates, and unemployment rates have resulted in an increasing number of Americans advocating protectionist policies to create a more favorable trade balance. Foreign competition is blamed for the problems in the weakest sectors of the economy, problems attributed to an uncontrolled surge in imports. These events have led to special interest groups lobbying for increased protection for selected American industries.[1] During the last 15 years, U.S. policy has been on a steady course toward protectionism. A policy to reduce tariffs across-the-board among all trading nations has been paralleled by efforts to protect selected industries from foreign competition. This paper assesses the role of specific interest groups in the movement toward protectionism.

The shift in U.S. policy toward bilateral trade arrangements under the rubric of fair trade makes U.S. policy more susceptible to pressure from special interest groups. Although there is a growing theoretical and empirical literature on this issue,[2] the interrelationship between the political and economic system and the influence of special interest groups is clearly a complex one. The analysis presented in this paper sheds some light on the economic determinants of trade restrictions across-the-board as well as restrictions in selected industries.

This paper is organized as follows. The first section presents a short historical overview of U.S. trade policy during the last two decades. This section documents the gradual shift in U.S. policy from an across-the-board free trade policy to one that focuses on bilateral fair trade. The second section presents a summary of the U.S. trade actions aimed at protecting specific industries during the 1960-1982 period. The third section discusses the data and estimation technique. The fourth section reports the empirical results and summary conclusions are presented in Section 5.

HISTORICAL OVERVIEW OF U.S. TRADE POLICY: THE MACRO EVENTS[3]

Following World War II, the United States was instrumental in the development of the General Agreement on Tariffs and Trade (GATT). This agreement is of particular interest since it established, among others, the following goals:

1. trade without discrimination (generalized, most favored nation treatment);
2. elimination of protection of domestic industry through tariffs.

Unfortunately, GATT allowed for "emergency" actions to serve as exceptions to the general rules (e.g., escape clauses). We call political actions having general trade effects "macro events."

U.S. trade policy throughout the 1960s was based on the GATT guidelines. It is not surprising that the largest number of trade actions affecting individual products by the United States were implemented through quantity restrictions, while macro events

Table 1. Summary of the Macro Events: 1960-1982

Date	*Event Description*
1962	*Trade Expansion Act of 1962:* President given authority to reduce tariffs of July 1, 1962, by 50 percent in five years; (1) allowed elimination of U.S. and European Economic Community together accounted for 80 percent of free world exports; (2) selected agricultural commodities where changes would assure some increase in U.S. exports of like goods; (3) tropical agricultural forestry products not produced in the United States if the European Economic Community would reciprocate; (4) articles which had an ad valorem rate of 5 percent.
	The Sixth GATT Tariff Conference: known as the Kennedy Round; authorized 50 percent tariff reductions on most industrial products and 30 percent to 50 percent on others.
1971	President Nixon orders the gold window closed and imposes an across-the-board 10 percent increase in tariffs (August).
1974	*Trade Act of 1974:* provides safeguards for American industry and American workers for unfair or injurious import competition; provided "adjustment assistance" for industries or workers hurt by imports.
1975	*Tokyo Round:* attempted to constrain nontariff barriers; negotiations designed to liberalize international trade. Since the most important negotiations were never implemented, the Tokyo Round will not be included in the list of events used in the empirical analysis.
1977	Canadian imports negotiated for first time (1977).
1979	*Trade Act of 1979:* overhauled U.S. countervailing duty laws which were designed to protect domestic industries against foreign government subsidies on imported goods; domestic industries required to show injury by subsidized imports before offsetting duty would be imposed; speeded investigations and imposition of penalties under countervailing duty and anti-dumping laws; established new customs valuation which used price actually paid for merchandise when sold for exportation to the United States; discouraged discrimination against foreign suppliers bidding for government purchase; curbing use of standards as disguised trade barriers.
1981	Embargoes on exports requiring validated licenses for shipment to Poland and the Soviet Union (1981).

across-the-board policy changes related to the nature of negotiations acceptable to Congress or exchange rate policies. A summary of the major trade macro events by the U.S. government is presented in Table 1 and a more extensive discussion of these macro events follows.

The enactment of the Trade Expansion Act of 1962 demonstrated the U.S. commitment to free trade. This legislation was the statutory mandate for the president to negotiate tariff cuts at the next GATT-sponsored multilateral trade negotiations, which were later to be called the Kennedy Round. The Kennedy Round had three objectives: (1) Overall reduction in tariffs, (2) Reduction of nontariff barriers, and (3) Participation of less developed countries. Import duties were cut an average of 35 percent on manufactured goods and 20 percent on agricultural products (excluding cereals, meat, and dairy products) as a result of the Kennedy Round. The reduction of nontariff barriers, on the other hand, was not as successful as had been hoped. The inability of the participants to reach agreement in the reduction of nontariff barriers anticipated many of the trade related problems of the 1970s.

In August 1971, President Nixon, in violation of the Bretton Woods agreement, refused to convert dollars into gold for foreign central banks. The dollar was devalued 8.6 percent relative to gold, making the official price of an ounce of gold 38 dollars. Tariffs were increased across-the-board by ten percent, and wage and price controls were imposed on the domestic economy. In December of that year, the tariff increase was rescinded and, under the Smithsonian agreement, the devaluation of the dollar against gold was "approved."[4]

Although free trade has been the self-described U.S. trade policy, policy has been shifting towards a new orientation based on "reciprocity." The objective of reciprocity is to force other nations to get rid of practices seen as injuring U.S. producers. Under this approach, if a nation failed to meet the reciprocity conditions, special restrictions and/or tariffs conceivably could be imposed on their export to the United States. The origins of this change in policy can be traced to the passage of the Trade Act of 1974. In response to industry and Congressional pressure, the Trade Act of 1974 was modified to include several provisions that eased the criteria necessary for imposing trade restraints. These included more flexible criteria for relief from increasing (but "fair") import competition, as well as substantive and procedural revisions of unfair trade practice laws, such as the antidumping and countervailing duty statutes.

In contrast to earlier statutes, the Trade Act of 1974 provides that an industry no longer need demonstrate that its injury was caused by imports resulting from an earlier tariff concession or that imports are even the "major" cause, that is, a cause no less important than any other cause, of its injury. Under the 1974 Act, it need only show that imports are a "substantial" cause. If the International Trade Commission (ITC) finds injury, the President then must consider what impact trade restrictions would have on the domestic economy, consumers, and the overall national interest. The final determination of what action, if any, should be taken is, essentially, at his discretion. The ITC may, however, recommend adjustment assistance instead of trade restrictions. If the President does not proclaim the relief recommended by the ITC, Congress may override the President and institute the relief recommended by the Commission.

Under the Trade Act on 1974, the authority of the President to impose quantity restrictions was increased. For the first time, the President was authorized to negotiate Orderly Marketing Agreements as a form of relief under the escape clause. The Act also required the fulfillment of reciprocity in trade concessions before a trade agreement could be binding between the United States and another major industrial country.

A SUMMARY OF THE RESTRICTIONS ON INDIVIDUAL COMMODITIES: THE MICRO EVENTS

Interventions in trade for individual industries are called "micro events" in this paper. A summary of micro events is provided in Table 2. We begin the history of micro events when President Nixon, in an effort to adhere to a 1968 campaign pledge, asked Japan and other countries to apply "voluntary" quotas on their exports of woolens and synthetic textiles to the United States. Since Japan was reluctant to abide by the "voluntary" quotas, the Chairman of the House Ways and Means Committee, Wilbur Mills, with encouragement from the Administration, introduced in May 1969 a bill to limit textile imports to their average annual level recorded in 1967 and 1968. This industry-specific trade policy is a micro event, in contrast to across-the-board macro events discussed in the previous section.

Table 2. Summary of the Micro Events: 1960-1982

Industry/SIC Code	*Trade Action (Date)*
Textiles (221, 222, 223)	Established voluntary quotas limiting the importation of cotton textiles (1961).
	Voluntary quota on exports to the United States of woolen and synthetic fabric (1968).
	Multifiber Arrangement—1974 restricted textile imports.
Sheet Glass & Carpets (227, 321)	Raised tariffs on sheet glass and carpets (1962).
Meat (02)	Meat Import Act of 1964 designed to protect domestic cattle industry; quotas come into effect when imports exceed adjusted base by 10 percent trigger level); President may elect to suspend quotas.
	Informal restraints on major meat supplying countries; special bilateral restrictions with Honduras (1969).
	Voluntary restraints on meat imports negotiated with additional countries (1970).
	Restraint program on meat continued which allowed for 1971 imports to be higher than the suspended trigger level but below negotiated restraint levels (1971).
	Voluntary restraints negotiated on meat (1972).
	Voluntary restraint negotiated on meat (1975).
	Voluntary restrictions on meat imports negotiated (1975).
Financial Institutions (60)	The Interest Equalization Tax (designed to restrict the availability to foreigners of banking services in the United States; mid-1960s).
	Foreign Direct Investment Program (designed to restrict U.S. financing of foreign direct investments by U.S. firms; mid-1960s).
Steel (331)	Voluntary Restraint Agreement imposed on imports of steel (1969).
	Voluntary Restraint Agreement on Steel extended from 1971 to 1974 (1972).
	Trigger Price Mechanism on steel implemented (1978).
	Steel quotas negotiated with European countries (1982).

(continued)

Table 2. (continued)

Industry/SIC Code	*Trade Action (Date)*
Specialty Steel (331)	Tariffs on stainless steel flatware raised (1971).
	Quotas placed on specialty steel (1976).
Fruit (017)	Negotiated voluntary quotas on Mexican fruit and vegetables (1971); allowed to lapse (1982).
Soybean (01)	U.S. soybean export embargo (1974).
Nonrubber Footwear (3149)	Orderly Marketing Agreement negotiated with Korea and Taiwan to restrict imports on nonrubber footwear to 1976 levels.
Color Televisions (3651)	Orderly Marketing Agreement with Japan to restrict import of color televisions (1977).
	Orderly Marketing Agreement with Korea and Taiwan to restrict imports of color televisions (1980).
Industrial Fasteners (345)	Restraints on imports of industrial fasteners (after once failing at the ITC) were imposed; the Commission was required to consider it again following Ways and Mean Committee request (1979).
Lightweight Chassis Trucks (3711)	25 percent tariff imposed on lightweight chassis trucks (1980).
Automobile (371)	"Voluntary" export restraints negotiated with Japan to restrict automobile imports (1980).
Motorcycles (375)	Harley Davidson seeks U.S. trade protection from Japanese imports (1982).

On January 1, 1969, the United States entered into Voluntary Restraint Agreements with countries exporting all types of steel into the United States. Domestic manufacturers of steel called for these restraints because they feared injury from the tremendous increase of imported steel.[5] These restrictions were in effect until December 31, 1971. A secondary set of "voluntary" restraints were imposed January 1, 1972, which extended the restrictions until December 31, 1974.

The Trade Act of 1974 triggered a rash of demands by U.S. industries for relief from import competition. These included requests for antidumping and countervailing duties, as well as escape clause restrictions on such items as chemical products, steel products, consumer electronics, industrial fasteners, canned hams, and vinyl shoes.

Unilateral changes in tariffs were specifically circumscribed by GATT. The agreement also sought to prohibit the use of quantitative restrictions, which were viewed as more harmful than tariffs. However, these prohibitions were not specific enough to prevent circumvention through quantitative restrictions that were quotas in all but name. And various kinds of nontariff barriers were introduced on a plethora of products. One of the most complex of these arrangements was the multifiber arrangements, establishing the parameters for restricting textile imports by the industrialized countries (effective January 1, 1974).

The use of a "Voluntary Export Restraints" to protect specific industries expanded during the 1970s. Under these arrangements, the importing country negotiates an agreement with the exporting country for that country to limit "voluntarily" the amounts of certain exports. In the United States, such negotiated trade restrictions, in the form of Orderly Marketing Agreements (OMAs), have been imposed on specialty steels, color television receivers, nonrubber footwear, certain meats, mushrooms, textiles, and automobiles.[6]

In 1976 the President obtained an Orderly Marketing Agreement to limit specialty steel exports from Japan and unilateral quotas were imposed on imports from the EEC and other countries. In March 1979, the U.S. International Trade Commission determined that Korean bicycle tires and tube imports were injuring domestic producers.[7] In October, the ITC recommended that President Carter impose three years of quotas on Russian anhydrous ammonia. In November, the Commission proposed a sharp increase in U.S. import duties on low priced porcelain-on-steel cookware. By late spring of 1980, pressure was building to impose significantly higher import duties on small trucks imported from Japan. In August 1980, that pressure resulted in a 25 percent duty on lightweight truck chassis originating from Japan.[8]

A significant increase in the use of trade restrictions as a foreign policy weapon was witnessed in 1980.[9] In response to the Soviet invasion of Afghanistan, the United States forbade domestic exporters to sell corn, wheat, and certain fertilizer products to the Soviet Union. Severe restrictions also were placed on the export of high technology products.

In the summer of 1980, Ford Motor Company joined with the United Auto Workers to petition the ITC to grant protection from import competition from Japan. The U.S. International Trade Commission determined that imports were not a substantial cause of the domestic auto industry's sales problem. Nonetheless, Congress and the Executive branch responded to political pressure, and "voluntary" export restraints were discussed with the Japanese government. In effect, the Japanese automakers, agreed, under pressure from the Japanese government, to restrict exports to the United States to 1.68 million units in the year following April 1981, and not to increase their exports unless the U.S. sales of all autos expand.

The move toward protectionism got another push when the domestic steel industry on January 11, 1982, filed forms with the Commerce Department and the International Commission, changing nine European countries, Brazil, and South Africa with unfair trade practices.

On October 21, just hours before the Commerce Department would have been required to impose countervailing and penalty duties—selective increases in U.S. tariffs and duties—quota negotiations were finalized limiting European steel imports to about 85 percent of 1981 levels.

EMPIRICAL ANALYSIS OF DETERMINANTS OF TRADE POLICY: SAMPLE SELECTION AND ESTIMATION TECHNIQUE

The historical review in the previous section suggests that interest groups use political pressure to force intervention in trade when their interests are served by reducing competition from abroad. The most important interest groups are labor and capital in the industry most affected by imports. On the other hand, macroeconomic developments of more general impact, such as a deterioration in the balance of trade, may provoke broader political interventions in trade patterns. The empirical analysis presented in this paper analyzes both the general macro event (across-the-board) restrictions, as well as on policies aimed at protecting individual industries, or micro events. Our analysis of the macro events relies on a time series analysis employing logit analysis. The analysis of micro events uses logit analysis with a mixture of cross section time series analysis.

To study changes in trade policy at the macroeconomic level, policy shifts are related to quantifications of the changes in the overall level of trade, employment, and the return to capital using logit analysis. Annual data on changes in the real balance of trade, employment, and the real rate of return on common stocks were related to the policy actions given in Table 1. A policy action having a generalized trade reducing effect in a given year is the event to be explained, and in that year the dependent variable takes the value of unity. Otherwise the dependent variable is zero. The period of analysis is 1960 to 1982, or 23 observations.

On the microeconomic level, trade restrictions imposed since 1960 were classified according to the Standard Industrial Classification (SIC) for the industry most affected by the trade restriction (as shown in Table 2). For each industry affected by a micro event trade, ten years of historical data on employment, imports, and return on capital were obtained. The sources for the employment and import measures were SIC classifications of employment in industries and imports. The Center of the Study of Security Prices (CRSP) file of returns by SIC code provided the industry average stock returns. After netting out industries for which inadequate data were available, eleven industries were included in the sample: they are listed in Table 3. In addition to the sample of industries directly affected by trade policy, a sample of six industries not affected by trade policy was selected at random and SICs for those are also given in Table 3.

The data for statistical analysis of micro effects were constructed from the sample of industries affected by trade policy as follows. First, the growth rates of employment and changes in growth rates

Table 3. Industry Classifications Used in Empirical Analysis

SIC Code	*Industry*	*SIC Code*	*Industry*
01	Agricultural Products	207	Fats & Oils
017	Fruits & Nuts	265	Paper Containers
222	Textiles (Synthetic)	394	Toys
223	Textiles (Wool)	2111	Tobacco (Cigarettes)
331	Steel	2732	Printing (Books)
2211	Textiles (Cotton)	3172	Leather Goods
2279	Carpets		
3149	Footwear (Nonrubber)		
3211	Flat Glass		
3651	Radio, TV Sets		
3711	Autos		

were computed for the two years prior to the intervention of trade policy. The growth rates were then expressed as the difference of the SIC industry employment growth from U.S. aggregate growth in employment and growth in SIC imports relative to total U.S. import growth. One observation consists, therefore, of the qualitative designation of trade intervention (typically a quota), the growth rate in employment and the relative change in the growth of imports expressed as differences from national averages, and the associated SIC industry stock return.

In addition to the above observations, the historical data from the affected industries and the matching sample were used to produce observations where no trade policy intervention occurred. With the historical series on affected industries, growth rates in employment and imports, again expressed as differences for U.S. averages, were computed for four and five years and seven and eight years prior to the trade policy intervention. With the firms from the matching sample, growth rates and returns were computed as with affected industries, where the time periods were staggered for the industries randomly and in some instances, due to data availability, five-year growth periods were used. The final sample micro event analysis was based on 60 observations.

The dependent variable in both the macro and micro event analysis was the qualitative variable indicating intervention or nonintervention or the imposition trade restrictions. Given the qualitative nature of the dependent variable, logit analysis was chosen to predict a policy of trade intervention given the measures of injury to industries affected by trade. The use of logit analysis is consistent with the use of this procedure in other applications (see Attiyeh for a survey of qualitative choice models). Logit has minimal requirements concerning the statistical properties of error terms in the regression. These requirements are met in the case of the political uncertainties associated with the intervention in trade which are the source of the stochastic error terms.

Logit analysis estimates a logistic probability curve as a function of the explanatory variables. Since the dependent variables are binary and the function is nonlinear, maximum likelihood estimation techniques are used. Our estimates are based on the Statistical Analysis System (SAS) logit routines for maximum likelihood estimation.

EMPIRICAL ANALYSIS: THE RESULTS

The results of estimating the logit model with all the explanatory variables are given in Table 4; Panel A gives the results of the macro event estimation, and Panel B the industry-specific or micro event results.

In the macro event analysis, the balance of trade term is significant, while the real stock return term is only marginally significant. The employment term is not significant. The interpretation of the estimated logit functions is that, whenever the real trade balance falls, the probability of a trade reducing policy initiative is increased. Broader effects of trade, such as reduced employment growth, are not associated with generalized trade reducing policy actions. This implies that generalized intervention in trade policy is most likely to occur with a deteriorating trade balance, which implies that ownership of domestic wealth is tending to be transferred abroad. This association of trade intervention with wealth transfers abroad is akin to the mercantilist point of view.

Several of the events deserve explanation. In particular, the embargoes to the Soviet Union and Poland in 1981 were political

Table 4. Results of Logit Estimation

Independent Variable	*Coefficient*	*Standard Error*	*Significance*
	A. Macro Trade-Reducing Policy Intervention (Dependent Variable = 0, 1)		
Intercept	-3.14	2.13	.139
Trade Balance as a Share of GNP	-4.22	1.89	.026
Real Stock Returns	-9.9	6.4	.124
Percent Change in Employment	-5.7	77.9	.940
Model Chi-Square	17.54		.0005
	B. Micro-Trade Reducing Policy Intervention (Dependent Variable = 0, 1)		
Intercept	-1.269	.356	.0004
Relative Growth in Employment in SIC	-9.616	5.37	.0732
Relative Growth in Imports in SIC	1.833	1.423	.1977
Stock Returns	-2.980	1.672	.0747
Model Chi-Square	8.10	Significance	.0394

events and might be excluded from the sample. However, during 1978 and 1981 the United States negotiated major trade restrictions on the import of steel and automobiles. In our empirical analysis we assumed that the United States did impose trade restriction in 1978 and 1981. In contrast, the 1975 Tokyo round negotiations are classified by us as non-event year for the reason that the most important negotiated concessions were never implemented.

In the specific industry analysis, the employment term proves to be the most significant explanatory variable, in marked contrast to the macro event results. Slow growth or decline in employment in affected industries relative to aggregate U.S. experience produces an increase in the probability of a trade reducing policy intervention which is significant at the 90 percent level. Nearly equal in significance is the stock return variable which are significant at the 90 percent level. This result no doubt reflects the fact that specific industry effects can be used to mobilize pressure from well-defined interest groups, such as labor and capital. The trade balance, in marked contrast to the marco results, has no statistically significant effect on the probability of trade interventions in a given industry, that is, on the micro event level.

The empirical results reported in the two panels of Table 4 are interesting, especially when compared to the results previously discussed in the literature. Most of the literature cited above uses ordinary least-squares cross-sectional analysis to estimate these effects. This makes the comparability of our results somewhat of a problem. In a recent paper Ray (1981) reports both ordinary least square and Probit cross-sectional analysis of U.S. trade restriction for the year 1970. Ray's results indicate that for specific industries (i.e., micro results) the percent change in imports does not play a significant role. This result is similar to the result reported below. Our macro event results suggest that the trade balance is a major determinant of macro across-the-board trade policy changes.

Ray's analysis uses a larger number of explanatory variables than ours (including capital intensity, concentration ratio, fraction of work force that is skilled), but in contrast to our analysis, he does not include a measure of total labor employment and/or profitability like the stock return variable we employ.

CONCLUSION

The intervention of policy in international trade appears to be systematically related to economic events according to our logit estimation. The interesting conclusion is that generalized or macro economic trade policy interventions are most immediately affected by wealth transfers, and not, as is usually assumed, to a slowing in employment growth. The major trade reducing policies since 1960 due to a deteriorating trade balance can be termed neomercantilism.

Specific industry trade policies are most significantly related to those interest groups directly affected by competition from abroad. Relatively slow growth or decline in employment in an industry tends to increase the probability of a policy reducing international trade in that industry as orderly marketing agreements or quotas are imposed to protect domestic employment. Shareholders' returns in those industries do not affect trade policy.

The movement from a commitment to free trade following World War II to so-called fair trade has meant an increasing use of specific trade restrictions. The legislative atmosphere for such intrusions into the free flow of goods has increased since the Trade Act of 1974. Given the significance of relative employment growth rates and the inevitability of dynamic changes in the employment in various sectors of the economy, pessimism concerning the future of free trade and the efficient allocation of resources across national boundaries may be warranted.

ACKNOWLEDGMENT

The authors notefully acknowledge the assistance of Vishwa Mudiliar, Adishura Jaim, and Deborah Mellard.

NOTES

1. For a discussion on the politics of special interest groups, see Brock and Magee (1978). The analysis of the rent seeking behavior can be traced to Krueger's (1974) seminal paper. Krueger's analysis has been further refined and generalized by Bhagwati and Srinivasan (1980).
2. An excellent summary of the theoretical and empirical literature can be found in Lavergne (1983).
3. This section draws heavily on Canto (1983).
4. For a discussion of the major trade issues at the time, see "U.S. Devalues Dollars 10% by Raising Price of Gold" (1973).
5. See the "The Attraction Quotas" (1969). For an analysis of the restrictions on the steel industry, see Canto (1984).
6. A more detailed analysis of the effects of the orderly marketing agreement on color televisions can be found in Canto and Laffer (1983).
7. See "U.S. Ruling Faults Imports of Korean Bicycle Tires" (1979).
8. See Pasztos (1980).
9. Support for these actions can be found in Allen (1980).

REFERENCES

Allen, F. 1980. "Executives Say Imports Pose Serious Threat." *Wall Street Journal* (August 27), p. 11.

Bhagwati, J.N., and Srinivasan, T.N. 1980. "Revenue Seeking: A Generalization of the Theory of Tariffs." *Journal of Political Economy* 88 (December): 1069-1087.

Brock, W.A., and Magee, S.P. 1978. "The Economics of Special Interest Politics: The Case of the Tariff." *American Economic Review Papers and Proceedings* 68 (May): 246-50.

Canto, V.A., and Laffer, A.B. 1983. "The Effectiveness of Orderly Marketing Agreements: The Color T.V. Case." *Business Economics* 18 (January): 38-45.

Canto, V.A. 1983. "U.S. Trade Policy: A Historical Perspective." *Canto Journal* 3, 3.

Canto, V.A. 1984. "The Effects of Voluntary Restraint Agreements: A Case Study of the Steel Industry." *Applied Economics.*

Krueger, A.O. 1974. "The Political Economy of the Rent Seeking Society." *American Economic Review* 64 (June): 291-303.

Lavergne, R.P. 1983. "The Political Economy of U.S. Tariffs." New York: Academic Press.

Pasztos, A. 1982. "Sharp Boost in Duties on Foreign Trucks is not Expected to Aid Sales of U.S. Models." *Wall Street Journal* (August 20), p. 90.

Ray, E.J. 1981. "The Determinants of Tariffs and Non-Tariffs Trade Restrictions in the United States." *Journal of Political Economy* 89(1): 105-121.

Ray, E.J. 1981. "Tariff and Non-Tariff Barriers to Trade in the United States and Abroad." *Review of Economics and Statistics* (May): 161-168.

"U.S. Devalues Dollars 10% by Raising Price of Gold." 1973. *Wall Street Journal* (February 13), p. 3.

"U.S. Ruling Faults Imports of Korean Bicycle Tires." 1979. *Wall Street Journal* (March 23), p. 36.

COMMENT ON "ECONOMIC DETERMINANTS OF U.S. TRADE POLICY: AN EMPIRICIAL ANALYSIS"

Tamir Agmon

Trade policy is to a large extent a political issue. Policy is determined by committees where both elected officials and public servants are making poicy decisions. They are aided by various depositions and testimonies presented by different interest groups. This is a political process. Yet much of the eocnomic research never leaves the premise of perfect market, where decisions are being made by "economic persons."

The paper by Canto and Dietrich is a useful attempt to merge the political considerations into an economic explanation of trade policy decisions. Moreover, they have embarked on the rather tricky road of quantifying the effect of political decisions, and relating it to economic explanatory variables. Indeed, the study provides an association between what the author dubbed "macro events" and economy-wide variables, such as a deterioration in the balance of trade, with industry-specific restrictions and industry-specific variables, such as a relative decline in employment. The authors stop short of providing a description and an analysis of the process by which changes in the chosen variables lead to the observed phenomenon of trade policies. They also do not discuss whether this process is an equilibrium process which is likely to continue. This last point is of particular importance to those who deal with planning, either in foreign or local firms, or in the relevant government departments. I will briefly address these two issues one by one below.

The idea of viewing trade policy, or for that matter any other set of government policies, as the outcome of pressures and other activities of various interest groups is not new. Krueger (1974) and Brock and Magee (1978) are just two of a number of research efforts which try to define this process. The question is what one does beyond the definition of the political process. Put in other words, is it possible to develop a model which will both satisfy the conceptual structure and be empirically testable? Even if such a model can be found, it is not likely to be unique.

Canto and Dietrich's study would be more complete had they addressed the conceptual part of their model and supplied the reader with an analysis regarding the operation of the interest groups and how they affect the distribution of relative prices.

This point is more relevant with regard to the macro events. The authors argue that in these cases the political response stems from the government at large, and they attribute this response to "neomercantilism." This argument is not consistent with the implied argumentation with regard to the industry restrictions. A possible conceptual approach can be derived from the agency theory, or from a game theoretic approach, which views the countries as the players.

The second extension of the work presented by Canto and Dietrich concerns the policy implications of their findings to both foreign and domestic firms. If a relative decline in the employment in a given industry increases the probability of a "trade action" by the United States with regard to the affected industry, this information has value. The exporting industry abroad may try to reduce the employment effect or to create a counter effect by creating employment. Such implications depend, however, on an additional testing with regard to the relationship between a relative decline in the employment in tradable industries in the United States and trade action. The results presented by Canto and Dietrich deal with the relations between trade action and a decline in the employment.

REFERENCES

Brock, W.A., and Magee, S.P. 1978. "The Economics of Special Interest Groups: The Case Tariffs." *American Economic Review* 68 (May): 246-250.

Krueger, A.O. 1974. "The Political Economy of the Rent Seeking Society." *American Economic Review* 64 (June): 291-303.

ON THE SYMMETRY BETWEEN EFFECTIVE TARIFFS AND VALUE ADDED SUBSIDIES

Edward Tower

ON ALTERNATIVE DEFINITIONS OF THE NOMINAL RATE OF PROTECTION

Thinking about the effective rate of protection is made difficult by the fact that the concept of the ERP has been used by different authors to refer to two different things, and sometimes by the same author to refer to different things. The confusion arises out of the fact that the nominal rate of protection (NRP) is not unambiguously defined. Corden (1971, pp. 21-25) notes that one can define the rate of protection as either (1) the proportional difference between the domestic (p) and foreign (p^*) prices of a good, $(p - p^*)/p^*$, or else (2) the proportional increase in the domestic price of a good that finally results from a protectionist regime. Of course when world prices are fixed both of these concepts are the same, but generaly they will be different. Corden goes on to say (p. 25), "Clearly, which concept one uses depends on one's purpose, but it is at least worth noting that the term *rate of protection* ... is not unambiguous. Generally the second meaning of the term is the one we shall have in mind when considering resource allocation effects of tariffs, export subsidies, and so on. But for *marginal* welfare analysis the first meaning is the relelvant one." This is true, and the same ambiguity applies to thinking about the ERP. I find the definition of the ERP which is analaogous to Corden's first definition of the NRP to be useful, because the ERP defined in this sense plays the role of a subsidy which is useful in welfare economics. However, I find the second definition to be much less useful. Thus, this paper presents implications of my preferred definition first, show some of what can be done with it, and then criticize the second definition.[1]

THEOREM AND IMPLICATIONS

There are two useful symmetry theorems regarding tariffs, taxes, and subsidies in international trade. One is the Lerner Symmetry Theorem, which states that across-the-board taxes on imports and across-the-board taxes on exports have identical effects.[2] The second is the proposition that an import tariff may be viewed as a combination of a consumption tax and a production subsidy.[3] In this paper we prove a third symmetry theorem closely related to the second:

> *Consider an economy which uses intermediate inputs in fixed proportions along with primary factors to produce outputs; all goods are traded internationally. In such an economy, there is an equivalence between two fiscal structures. One is the levy of a vector of tariffs on net imports, where these tariffs are expressed as fractions of world prices. The other is the levy of a set of consumption taxes (expressed as fractions of prices to sellers) equal to that set of nominal tariffs combined with a set of subsidies to value-added (expressed as a fraction of gross value added), equal to the effective rates of protection (ERPs), where these ERPs are calculated as the proportion by which unit value-added at domestic prices exceeds unit value added at world prices, with both measures determined using the domestic physical input-output coefficients.*

This theorem is rather general, for it holds in both barter and monetary economies and it holds whether or not world prices are fixed, but like the invalence between tariffs and quotas it does require that markets be competitive. It is also a theorem which is closely related to statements in the literature.[4] Still, it has never been stated, and I believe it provides a useful way of looking at the ERP.[5]

Moreover, the theorem has an important neutrality theorem as a corollary which is:

> *A vector of tariffs on net imports combined with the same vector of consumption subsidies (expressed as fractions of the prices to consumers) and taxes on value added (expressed as fractions of disposable factor incomes) equal to the implied ERPs will be equivalent to free trade.*

From a policy standpoint, the corollary is very important. The World Bank frequently calculates effective rates of protection. But ERPs have fallen into ill repute in some quarters because they are imperfect indicators of how freeing up trade would move resources or affect economic welfare.[6] But this is noit a proper reason to reject such calculations, because after all even when there is no input-output structure, tariff changes are not perfect predictors of welfare changes or resource movements,[7] yet it is useful to know what tariffs are, for they are essential inputs into any general equilibrium calculation. Similarly, ERPs play an important role in many general equilibrium calculations designed to reach conclusions about both welfare and resourcer allocation,[8] for they can be thought of as implicit subsidy rates on value added, and hence the distortion associated with employment of resources in a particular activity.

I conclude, therefore, that policy advisors may find it helpful to interpret ERPs as the equivalents of value-added subsidies, and the normative significance they should attach to differential ERPs is precisely the normative significance that one would attach to differential subsidies and taxes on value added in different sectors: namely a value-added subsidy is the amount by which the wage received by the suppliers of factors exceeds the wage paid by demanders of factors.

Competition causes the supply prices of the same factor in all industries to be the same. Therefore, differential subsidies to value added will cause the subsidy-inclusive costs of the same factors to different demanders to differ by the subsidy differential. Thus, we can treat the ERP as the distortion associated with the production of value added, which means that the policymaker need only point out that differential ERPs are production distortions, and that to eliminate the distortions on production, differential value-added taxation can be used to offset completely the ERPs; and similarly to eliminate the distortions on consumption, differential consumption subsidies can be used to offset completely the nominal tariffs. Moreover, such a complete offset occurs when consumption subsidies (as a fraction of the prices to consumers) are levied at the nominal tariff rates and value added in all industries is taxed at a rate (as a fraction of disposable income) equal to the effective rate of protection.

DEFINING THE ERP AND EXPLORING ITS RELATIONSHIP TO THE NRP

We use the conventional assumption that intermediate inputs and a value-added aggregate are combined in fixed proportions and with constant returns to scale (CRS) to produce output, and that the value-added aggregate is itself a CRS aggregate of primary factors (e.g., capital and labor).

Given our assumed production relatinship, any activity can be thought of as the production of a basket of various goods in fixed proportions, where some of the goods are present in the basket in negative quantities (i.e., as inputs). The value of the basket in world prices is simply value added measured in world prices. Similarly, the value of the basket in domestic prices is simply value added in domestic prices.

Gorden's first definition of the NRP of a good is simply the proportion by which its domestic price exceeds its world price. If the good is an importable, this is simply the nominal tariff rate expressed as a fraction of the world price, and if it is an exportable it is simply the export subsidy again expressed as a proportion of the world price. By analogy, we choose to define the ERP as simply the proportion by which the domestic price of the basket exceeds the world price. The ERP for an activity then is the average tariff on the items in the particular commodity basket produced by that activity. Therefore, it is not surprising that it plays a role which is similar to that of the NRP. Moreover, in the special case where there are no intermediate inputs, this definition boils down to that of the NRP.

THE EQUIVALENCE PROPOSITION

Let us define the following terms:

- p^p_i is the price of good i to producers of good i.
- a_{ij} is an input-output coefficient for the domestic economy expressed in physical units.
- e_i is the ad valorem excise tax on sales of good i to consumers, expressed as a fraction of p^p_i.
- p^c_i is the price of good i to consumers of good i.
- VAS_i is the value-added subsidy on the production of good i expressed as a fraction of gross payments to primary factors in industry i.
- p^*_i is the international price of good i.
- t_i is the proportion by which the price of good i to domestic producers of good i exceeds its world price. Thus for tradable goods with binding border taxes t_i will be i's import tariff or export subsidy.
- v^g_i is unit value added in industry i at domestic prices calculated gross of any tax or subsidy on value added and v^g_i is defined as $p^p_i - \sum_j a_{ji}p^p_j$. Thus it is the price of a basket of goods produced by activity i, where the basket's size is defined so that it contains one unit of good i.
- v^d_i is disposable income accruing to the primary factors of production in industry i per unit of output produced. Thus, it is unit value added at domestic prices inclusive of any subsidy to value added or net of any tax on it.

v^*_i is unit value added at international prices using domestic physical input-output coefficients, and v^*_i is defined as $p^*_i - \sum_j a_{ji}p^*_j$.

Whether good i is traded or not it will be true that:

$$p^c_i = (1 + e_i)p^p_i \tag{1}$$

If good i is either imported or exported:

$$p^p_i = (1 + t_i)p^*_i \tag{2}$$

Thus for traded goods (1) and (2) yield:

$$p^c_i = (1 + e_i)(1 + t_i)p^*_i \tag{3}$$

Finally,

$$v^d_i = (1 + \text{VAS}_i)\, v^g_i \tag{4}$$

Let us define the effective protection of value added as:

$$\text{ERP}_i = \frac{v^g_i - v^*_i}{v^*_i} \tag{5}$$

which is consistent with the definition of Balassa and Associates (1982, p. 352). Then we can use Equation (4) to rewrite Equation (5) as:

$$v^d_i = (1 + \text{VAS}_i)(1 + \text{ERP}_i)v^*_i \tag{6}$$

Since e_i and t_i play a symmetric role in Equation (3) and ERP_i and VAS_i play a symmetric role in Equation (6), it is clear that the theorem holds with competition and no nontraded goods.

Moreover, when we define consumption subsidies (s_i) as fractions of prices to consumers, instead of Equation (3) we have:

$$p^c_i (1 + s_i) = (1 + t_i)p^*_i \tag{7}$$

so:

$$p_i^c = \left[\frac{1 + t_i}{1 + s_i}\right] p_i^* \tag{8}$$

Similarly, when we define value-added taxes (VAT_i) as fractions disposable value added, instead of Equation (6) we have:

$$v_i^d(1 + VAT_i) = (1 + ERP_i)\, v_i^* \tag{9}$$

so

$$v_i^d = \left[\frac{1 + ERP_i}{1 + VAT_i}\right] v_i^* \tag{10}$$

Equations (8) and (10) illustrate the corollary, still assuming competition and no nontraded goods.

Itis easy to see the logic of these two ideas using the simply diagram in Figure 1. All gods are traded at fixed world prices. *D* shows the domestic demand for the good in question. The only input is good *j*, and a_j as its input coefficient. Thus EE′ shows the cost of the sole intermediate input per unit of output at world price. *v* is drawn with respect to EE′ as the horizontal axis and is the supply curve of value-added. In free trade domestic output is at G with consumption at H. A tariff on the import of *i* raises domestic price by AC to A so that consumption falls to H′, which is just as if a consumption tax of AC had been imposed. The import tariff on *j*, T_j, raises unit costs by AB, so the next increase in unit value added at domestic prices is only BC. This means that production equilibrium moves to G′, with unit value added at domestic and world prices given by v_i = BE and v_i^* = CE respectively. Thus, the ERP is given by BC/CE. However the same result on the supply side could have been brought about by free trade combined with a proportion subsidy to gross value added (i.e., value added before the subsidy) of BC/CE. Thus the equivalence is established. Similarly, an import tariff on *i*of AC combined with a consumption subsidy of AC restores consumption to H, while our set of tariffs combined with a tax on unit

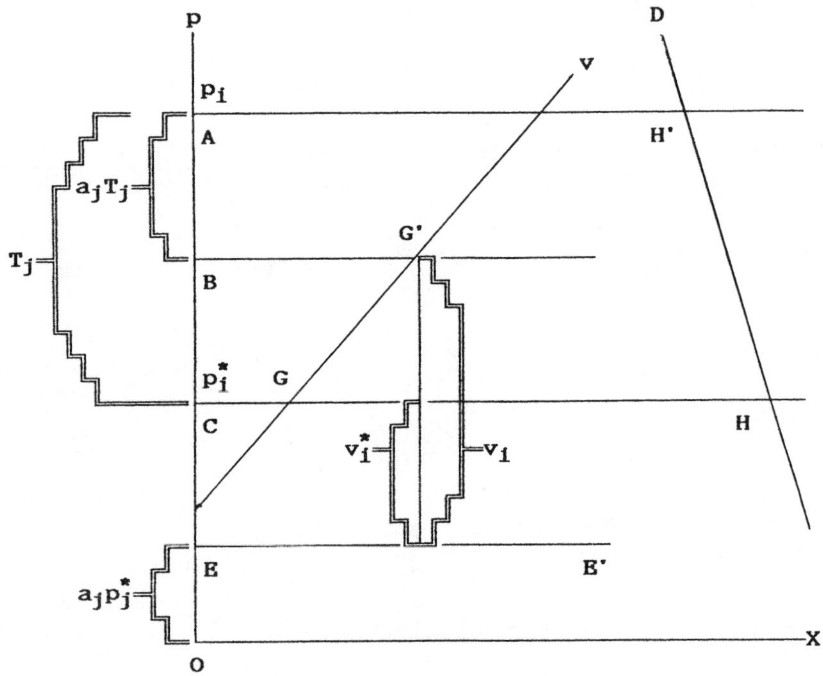

Figure 1. The Equivalence Proposition Illustrated

value added of BC restroes production equilibrium to G, and this establishes our neutrality theorem.

ADDITIONAL EQUIVALENCE PROPOSITIONS

There are two additional equivalence propositions which further clarify the meaning of the ERP, although they are not as useful as the ones we have just discussed. We have defined the ERP as the wedge between the domstic price of a sector's basket of goods and world price created by the tariff structure. It is a small additional step to note that if all of a sector's inputs and outputs were subject to an import tariff or export subsidy equal to the ERP calculated from the existing tariff structure, instead of their actual tariffs, no real variables would change. Thus, the ERP is the average tariff on an activity's inputs and outputs. This gives us yet another equivalence proposition:

> *Consider an economy which uses intermediate inputs in fixed proportions along with primary factors to produce outputs. In such an economy, there is an equivalence between two fiscal structures. One is the levy of a vector of tariffs on net imports, where these tariffs are expressed as frctions of world prices. The other is the levy of a set of consumption taxes (expressed as fractions of prices to sellers) equal to that set of nominal tariffs combined with a set of taxes on each sector's inputs and subsidies on its outputs (expressed as a fraction of world prices) equal to its effective rate of protection.*

Moreover, we can come up with an equivalence proposition that holds even when there is substitution in use of intermediate inputs:

> *Consider an economy which uses intermediate inputs in variable proportionss but with constant returns to scale along with primary factors to produce outputs. In such an economy, there is an equivalence between two fiscal structures. One is the levy of a vector of tariffs on net imports, where these tariffs are expressed as fractions of world prices. The other is the levy of a set of consumption taxes (expressed as fractions of prices to sellers) equal to that set of nominal tariffs combined with a set of subsidies to value added equal to the ERPs and a set of taxes on each of a sector's net inputs equal to the initial tariff minus the sector's ERP.*[9]

Thus, the ERP still has a meaning as an indicator of incentives even with substitution between intermediate inputs, but it is questionable whether anyone would find the concept very useful in these circumstances.

THE EFFECTIVE RATE OF VALUE-ADDED SUBSIDY AND THE IMPLICIT RATE OF FINAL DEMAND TAXATION

From the standpoint of policy modeling perhaps the most important dividend of this discussion is that one can write the relationship between world prices and prices to final demanders of traded goods as:

$$p_i^c = (1 + \tau_i)p_i^* \tag{11}$$

and label τ_i as the implicit rate of final demand taxation, because it is the proportion by which prices to final demanders are raised above world prices by the tax and tariff structure.

Similarly,

$$v_i^d = (1 + z_i)v_i^* \tag{12}$$

where z_i is the effective rate of value added subsidy because it is the amount by which disposable value added, v_i^d, exceeds what it would be if inputs and outputs were evaluated at world prices, v_i^*. Substituting from Equations (3) and (6) into these equations yields expressions of these two rates:

$$\tau_i = (1 + e_i)(1 + t_i) - 1 \tag{13}$$

and

$$z_i = (1 + \text{VAS}_i)(1 + \text{ERP}_i) = 1 \tag{14}$$

Since the incentive system can be completely described by τ_i and z_i, these last two formulae are useful summaries of the incentives yielded by any tax or tariff system for use in policy analysis.[10]

Finally, it is important not to focus solely on the effective subsidization of value added to the exclusion of implicit final demand taxation. It is important to know both things in order to fully describe the incentives present. Since there is more scope for specialization in production than in consumption, the former are more important than the latter, but it would be a mistake to entirely ignore the latter.

NONTRADED GOODS

Nontraded goods as inputs and/or outputs create no problem for our equivalence propositions. If they are potentially tradeable, our equations hold with t_i defined from Equation (2) as $(p^p_i - p^*_i)/p^*_i$, the wedge between domestic producer prices and world prices.

Finally, when there are truly nontraded goods, which would not be traded even in the absence of trade barriers, we have four standard options, which I have embellished to account for nontraded final goods.

The "Sophisticated" Corden Method

THe first option is to treat any production process, along with its associated nontraded inputs, as an integrated production process which uses traded inputs and primary factors to produce outputs. This is the Corden method (referred to by Little, Scitovsky, and Scott, 1970, as the "sopphisticated" Corden method to distinguish it from the "crude" Corden method explained below) of treating nontraded goods. It is described in Balassa et al. (1982, pp. 352-353). Throughout the rest of the paper, in defining the ERP of a nontraded good, i, we set $p^*_i = p^p_i$. In this case, assuming zero initial consumption taxes, the observed tariff structure is equivalent to free trade plus:

1. a set of consumption taxes on tradeables equal to that set of nominal tariffs, plus
2. zero consumption taxes on nontradables plus
3. a set of subsidies to value added in the integrated tradeables industries equal to their ERPs plus
4. a set of subsidies to value added in the integrated nontradeables industries which produce solely for domestic consumption equal to their ERPs. Thus, in this scheme, production of a nontraded good which uses no nontraded inputs, and is both consumed directly and used as an input into the production of another good, is counted as one production process and as part of another.

The Balassa Method

A second option for treating nontraded goods is the Balassa method described in Balassa et al. (1982, pp. 352-353). Using this method we define the Balassa ERP by Equation (5) with the terms in the right hand side of Equation (5) defined as:

$$v^*_i + H_i = p^*_i - \sum_j a_{ji} p^*_i \tag{15}$$

and

$$v^g_i + H_i = p^p_i - \sum_j a_{ji} p^p_j \tag{16}$$

where we assume away any initial value added taxation so that, virutally, $v_i = v^d_i = v^g_i$; a_{ji} consists of the physical measure of the jth tradeable used directly in producing a unit of i and indirectly in producing the nontradeables that go into producing a unit of i; H_i is value added in producing nontradeables (home goods) used directly and indirectly in producing a unit of i; and v^*_i, v^d_i, v^g_i, and v_i refer to value added in the ith industry narrowly defined, that is, not vertically integrated as in the Corden method.

Then, combining Equations (15) and (16) with Equations (4) and (5), we can produce Equation (6) as before, which indicates the symmetry between the Balassa ERP and value added subsidization. Thus, if we observe a particular set of v^*_i, H_i, v^d_i, p^*_i, $\sum_j a_{ji}p^*_j$, $\sum a_{ji}p^p_i$, for some i, and are told there are no value-added taxes, we can calculate the Balassa ERP associated with it. If, alternatively, we are confronted with the same data on v^d_i and v^*_i and are told that there are no tariffs and no value added taxes on intermediate nontraded goods, we can calculate the value added subsidy on good i which is consistent with the data, and this subsidy will be the Balassa ERP for good i.

Thus the Balassa ERP for good i is the subsidy to value added in i which has the same impact on all real variables as the tariff on i and on its direct and indirect inputs, under the assumption that there is no value added taxation on the nontradeables used as intermediate inputs.

Clearly, then, there is a symmetry between a set of tariffs and zero consumption taxes on the one hand, and on the other free trade plus

1. a set of consumption taxes on tradeables equal to the nominal tariffs, plus
2. zero consumption taxes on nontradeables, plus
3. value added subsidies equal to the Balassa ERPs on the production of both all tradeables and those nontradeables which are directly consumed, plus
4. zero value added subsidies on nontradeables used as intermediate inputs.

The 'Crude' Corden Method

A third option for treating nontraded goods is the "Crude" Corden method described in Little, Scitovsky, and Scott (1970, pp. 431-432). Using this method we define the crude Corden ERP by Equation (5) with the terms in the right hand side defined as:

$$v^*_i = p^*_i - \sum_j a_{ji} p^*_j \qquad (17)$$

and

$$v^g_i = p^p_i - \sum_j a_{ji} p^p_i \qquad (18)$$

where a_{ji} consists of the physical measure of the jth tradeable used directly in producing a unit of i. Thus, in this method we treat nontradeable inputs into i just like primary factors in calculating value added, and hence the ERP. The difference between this method and the "sophisticated" Corden method is that, in the former, we do not net out traded inputs into nontraded goods in calculating value added.

With this definition, there is a symmetry between a set of tariffs and zero consumption taxes on the one hand, and on the other free trade plus

1. a set of consumption taxes on tradables equal to that set of nominal tariffs, plus
2. zero consumption taxes on nontradables, plus
3. subsidies on the use of primary factors and nontradables to produce tradeables and nontradeables equal to the crude Corden ERPs.

The reader should note that these definitions of the Balassa and Corden methods deviate a bit from those authors' definitions, because in their work, their reference prices are free trade prices rather than world prices. Our procedure has been to choose definitions that fit the symmetry theorems.

The Simple Balassa Method

A fourth option is labeled by Corden (1975, p. 64) the simple Balassa method.[11] This is to set $p^*_i = p^p_i$ for all nontraded goods in the calculation of effective protection of all traded and nontraded goods. In words, the reference price for each nontraded good, p^*_i, is simply the price which the domestic producer receives for it. Then we treat an excise tax on the sale of the *j*th good to the *i*th producer just like a tariff on the *j*th good in calcualting the ERP on *i*. Thus, the ERP on nontraded good which uses nontraded goods as its sole intermediate inputs woulod be the (negative) value added subsidy which is equivalent to the excise taxes paid on its intermediate inputs of nontraded goods. Corden (1984) notes that we can define a scale of ERPs for all tradeables, but this fourth definition, like the other three, enables us to calculate an ERP for each traded and nontraded good, and in calculating ERPs using this definition one need look only at direct inputs. Thus, in contrast to the sophisticated Corden and first Balassa methods, no matrix inversion is required.[12]

The symmetry theorem which emerges in this case is relatively simple:

> *Consider an economy which uses intermediate inputs in fixed proportions along with primary factors to produce outputs. In such*

an economy, there is an equivalence between two fiscal structures. One is the levy of a vector of nominal tariffs on net purchases, where these tariffs are expressed as fractions of reference prices which are world prices for tradables and prices to sellers for nontradeables. The other is the levy of a set of consumption taxes (expressed as fractions of prices to sellers) equal to that set of nominal tariffs combined with a set of subsidies to value-added (expressed as a fraction of gross value aded), equal to the effective rates of protection, where these ERPs are calculated as the proportion by which unit value-added at prices t othe sector exceeds unit value added at reference prices, with both measures determined using the domestic physical input-output coefficients.

Finally, selecting a reference price of p^p_i for nontraded goods is completely arbitrary. The symmetry and neutrality theorems will hold regardless of what price is selected. It is just that when a higher reference price for good i is selected, the ERPs for goods which use i as an intermediate input will be larger and the ERP for good i will be lower thani they would otherwise.

These ERPs represent wedges rather than measures of incidence. For example, if an intermediate nontraded input is provided inelastically with nontaxed intermediate inputs, and an excise tax is imposed on it, producers of that good would bear the incidence of the tax, although the tax would leave its ERP, as we propose to calculate it, still at zero and would reduce the algebraic value of the ERPs of the sectors which use it.

MONOPOLY POWER

So far we have ducked the problem of monopoly power. Imperfect competition in either the home or foreign economy will destroy the symmetry of the theorem in its most simple form. The problem is that if the monopolist-monopsonist is not a price taker in either his output market or the market for his intermediate inputs, a given set of nominal tariffs will generate different levels of the calculated ERP depending on what level of output the monopolist-monopsonist chooses. Thus, for the monopolist-monopsonist, ERP will be a function of his level of output:

$$\text{ERP}_i = \text{ERP}_i(Q_i) \tag{19}$$

Accordingly, for our monopolist-monopsonist, a symmetry emerges, but it is a symmetry between the effective rate of protection and a subsidy to value added which has the same functional dependence on output that ERP does:

$$\text{VAS}_i = \text{ERP}_i(Q_i) \tag{20}$$

In the special case where our monopolist-monopsonist is unable to influence the price of any of his inputs or the price of his output, it is not necessary to reckon with the monopoly-monopsony behavior explicitly, and the symmetry theorem which holds under competition continues to hold under monopoly.

ABSOLUTE LEVELS OF NOMINAL AND EFFECTIVE PROTECTION DON'T MATTER

If we ignore capital flows between countries, pretend that either the exchange rate or wages and prices are perfectly flexible, and assume that the government's real budget surplus is kept constant by a variable neutral income subsidy, absolute domestic prices cease to play a role, and only relative domestic prices matter. In that circumstance, if we use one of the two Corden methods to deal with nontraded goods and no nontraded goods are consumed, any fiscal structure (sets of e, t, VAS and ERP) will be equivalent to any initial fiscal structure (sets of $\bar{e}$, $\bar{t}$, $\overline{\text{VAS}}$, and $\overline{\text{ERP}}$) so long as relative prices stay unchanged, that is, from Equations (3) and (6), so long as for all i:

$$(1 + e_i)(1 + t_i) = \alpha(1 + \bar{e}_i)(1 + \bar{t}_i)$$

$$\text{and} \tag{21}$$

$$(1 + \text{VAS}_i)(1 + \text{ERP}_i) = \beta(1 + \overline{\text{VAS}}_i)(1 + \overline{\text{ERP}}_i)$$

where α and β are arbitrary positive factors of proportionality. Thus, for example, we can double the "force"[13] of each ERP and nominal tariff and/or triple the force of each excise tax without affecting any real variable.[14] This mans that policy advisors, when talking with clients, should emphasize that uniformly positive ERPs mean only that domestic prices will be absolutely higher than foreign ones, but in a barter world or in a nonbarter world in equilibrium with no price rigidities, the only thing that matters is the ratios of the forces of the ERPs.[15]

THE NET EFFECTIVE RATE OF PROTECTION

The irrelevence of absolute ERPs has led Corden (1966) to introduce the concept of the net effective rate of protection, NERP, where the ERP is simply the proportional change due to the tariff structure in value added measured in units of a basket of nontraded goods. Thus, the NERP is a device for normalizing ERPs. In general, the choice of the basket of goods to use as numeraire is somewhat arbitrary. However, in the special case where value added in every sector is produced with one sector specific factor an a common mobile factor, for example, labor, the WAGE of themobile factor is the natural choice for numeraire, for then the mobiel factor will have moved in or out of the sector in accordance with whether the sign of the NERP is positive or negative. Equal ERPs in all sectors will result in uniformly zero NERPs.

Balassa (1982, p. 353) describes the NERP as correcting for the currency appreciation which typically accompoanies the imposition of a tariff structure. However, this is confusing because the appreciation that occurs depends on which basket of goods has its domestic currency price held constant by domestic monetary policy, and this is arbitrary.[16]

Finally, Corden (1971, p. 162) discusses yet another way of treating nontraded goods, the Scott method, which requires treating nontraded goods like traded goods in calculating value added where in calculating ERPs, the increase in the world price of the nontraded good due to the tariff structure is treated just like a tariff which raises the domestic price of a traded good. Denoting N as the proportional increase in the price of the nontraded good due to the tariff structure, and SERP as the Scott measure of the ERP of a good, we can solve for the net ERP (NERP) as:

$$1 + \text{NERP} = \frac{1 + \text{SERP}}{1 + N}.$$

Thus, the relationship between the Scott method and the NERP is very close. Both are attempts to solve the general equilibrium problem, and while the numeraire in the Scott method is world prices, in the NERP it is the price of some bundle of nontraded goods.

NEGATING THE REAL IMPACT OF A TARIFF STRUCTURE

Equations (8) and (10) indicate that proportionality between consumer prices and world prices and between domestic and world value added is maintained which means that there are no consumption or production distortions, so long as for all i:

$$\frac{1 + t_i}{1 + s_i} = \gamma \quad \text{and} \quad \frac{1 + \text{ERP}_i}{1 + \text{VAT}_i} = \epsilon \tag{22}$$

where γ and ϵ are arbitrary positive factors of proportionality. Thus, it is possible to offset completely the consequences for resource allocation, and hence real income of an existing tariff structure, with various sets of consumption subsidies and production taxes so long as the forces of the consumption subsidies are proportional to the forces of the nominal tariffs and the forces of the value added taxes are proportional to the forces of the effective tariffs.

ON NEUTRALITY WHEN THERE IS SUBSTITUTABILITY BETWEEN INTERMEDIATE INPUTS

We have established that when intermediate input coefficients are fixed, the effects of a tariff structure on production can be completely offset by taxing value added at a rate equal to the ERP. What happens when there is substitutability between intermediate inputs? Is there an analogous theorem? The answer is yes.

Suppose there is substitutability between inputs. Moreover, suppose that the tax authority calculates the ERP for each firm and imposes a tax, VAT, on its value added equal to its ERP. This means that we have:

$$v_i^d(1 + \mathrm{VAT}_i) = p_i - \sum_j a_{ji} p_i \tag{23}$$

and

$$1 + \mathrm{ERP}_i = \frac{p_i - \sum_j a_{ji} p_j}{p^*_i - \sum_j a_{ji} p^*_j} \tag{24}$$

Combining Equations (23) and (24) with $\mathrm{ERP}_i = \mathrm{VAT}_i$ yields:

$$v_i^d = p^*_i - \sum a_{ji} p^*_j \tag{25}$$

Thus, we see that with value added taxed at the ERP, disposable value added depends solely on input coefficients and world prices. Thus, the firm will select a level of output and blend of inputs which is independent of the tariffs it pays on inputs and receives on its output. This is because it realizes that if it buys more of a heavily tariffed input, its ERP will fall, and consequently so will its value added tax, leaving it with increased costs equal to the value of the increased input at world prices.

Clearly, then, if there are no nontraded goods, we can achieve production efficiency by taxing value added in each industry at a rate equal to its ERP.

Moreover, nontraded goods cause no problem. Define p^* for nontraded goods as being equal to p. Then we have a symmetry theorem which states:

> *There is no economic difference between free trade on the one hand, and on the other a set of tariffs just balanced by consumption subsidies equal to those tariffs and value added taxes levied on each firm (regardless of whether it uses and/or produces tradable or nontradable goods) equal to its own ERP, and this is true even in the presence of monopoly-monopsony power, variable world prices, variable input-output coefficients for intermediate goods, a fixed exchange rate, inflexible factor prices in real or nominal terms, and trade imbalance.*

The reason that the symmetry holds even when there is a fixed exchange rate and inflexible factor prices is that substituting the one policy for the other causes no nominal price faced by consumers or factors of production to alter.

ON DRAWBACKS

Even aside from the formal symmetry developed here, there is an important moral which emerges. Many countries permit exporters who use imported inputs to draw back the tariffs they have paid. Generally, this is argued to be a good idea because it restores the competitiveness of the exporters. But there is a second resaon why this is a good idea. It encourages thm to choose an import mix as if they faced world prices rather than domestic prices for those imports. Thus, even if industries were homogenous entities it would be better on this ground to offer drawbacks or to tax at ERPs calculated from firm data than to tax at ERPs based on industry-wide data on import use.

ON A PROPOSAL TO LIBERALIZE TRADE

Now let us see how some of these ideas can be used to facilitate trade liberalization. Let us pretend once again that output is produced using various factors in fixed proportions and initially assume away nontraded goods. If a country wished to liberalize trade without affecting the income of any factor adversely it could immediately abolish all import restrictions, and simultaneously initiate value added subsidies equal to the EPs. Such a policy would result in a consumption gains from trade, without causing any factors to move between sectors. Moreover, factor incomes would remain unchanged. If all factors have identical tastes and unitary income elasticities of demand for all commodities, they would share identical proportional increases in their real incomes. More generally, so long as the budget shares in consumption of all the factors are reasonably equal, we would expect all factors to experience roughly the same proportionate change in real income. Then, through time, the country could move its value added taxes to uniformity. Probably a reasonable scheme would be to fix a future time period, say five years in the future, by which full equality would be achieved, with 20 percent of the initial discrepancy in each of the taxes eliminated in each year of the transition.

Nontraded goods would casue no conceptual difficulties. The only problem is that to find the level of value added taxation that would freeze their initial output levels and hence factor incomes, it would be necessary for the government to pick norms for disposable factor incomes and be prepared to tax or subsidize as needed to bring incomes in line with those norms.

Such a proposal would be second best to many that could be devised, but I believe it would be preferable to the traditional method of tariff reduction, which is to gradually reduce tariffs, and it recognizes that if the policymaker's goal is to avoid rapid changes in income distribution between industries, the best policy is value added taxation and subsidization, not tariffs.

Of course, to the extent that the same domestic and foreign product may not be perfect substitutes, abolishing tariffs could cause changes in the prices that domestic goods would fetch. Still, we could deal with this problem as with nontraded goods, namely, adjust the value added subsidy.[17]

OTHER DEFINITIONS OF THE EFFECTIVE RATE OF PROTECTION

Throughout this paper we have interpreted the ERP as a measure of the implicit subsidy to value added. However, other authors have used other definitions which are analogous to Corden's second definition of the NRP, and they have used the ERP for other purposes. In this section we examine these other definitions and uses.

Bhagwati and Srinivasan (1983) write:

> The objective of ERP theory, then consists in devising a concept of protection that, in the presence of tariff structures involving the imports of intermediate goods, constitutes in effect an index that will perform the same tasks nominal tariffs perform in nominal tariff theory: predicting accurately the changes in gross output, primary factor allocation, real value added, and/or nominal value added. (p. 127)

They continue:

> Two basic definitions of an ERP index have developed in the literature. In Corden 1966 and Anderson and Naya 1969 it is defined as the proportionate increment in value added per unit level of an activity brought about by the tariff struckture over its free-trade value, whereas in Corden 1969 and Leith 1968 it is defined as the proportionate change (due to the tariff structure) in the "price" of value added (with the assumption that such a "price" can be defined meaningfully). (p. 127)
>
> . . .
>
> The two definitions generally yield different ERP numbers. However, in the special case of a separable production function where the intermediates are used in fixed proportion to output, both definitions amount to the same thing. (p. 129)

Thus, in their view the ERP is interesting only to the extent that it is correlated with the change, due to the tariff structure, in other variables of interest. Clearly, if we were to solve a general equilibrium system to determine the impact of a tariff structure on real incomes of various groups and levels of outputs in various sectors, the concept of the ERP would be superfluous, and it would be sensible to concur with Dixit (1985) who writes:

> To sum up, Samuelson's dictum about consumer surplus seems to apply equally well to effective protection: the concept can safely be used only by those who understand it sufficiently well to do without it. (section 6.2)

Harberger (undated) on the other hand lists the theory of effective protection as one of the four major developments in economic theory which has contributed to the changes that took place in the economics profession's view of the development process in the past few decades. He notes that this is becuase "empirical studies ... have shown first how high, typically, the effetive rates of protection are, and second how heavy are the burdens, in terms of the resulting inefficiency, that many developing countries have, as it were, imposed upon themselves." He also writes, "All the confusion about what the rate of effective protection is can be avoided only by having a uniform and general tariff on all imports. So while the first lesson emerging from effective protection and analysis is 'liberalize,' the second is, to the extent that liberalization is incomplete, 'equalize' the tariff schedule."

I propose that we drop the use of the ERP as defined in thet wo senses considered by Bhagwati and Srinivasan, and replaced it with the concept of the ERP defined as a measure of the tax or subsidy incentive to the value added discussed earlier in this section. Then, if desired, these incentive measures can be combined with other parameters to calculate the impact of protection on important variables. Moreover, the ERP defined in this way is easier to calculate and, I suspect, will be correlated almost as closely in most circumstances with variables of importanceas the Bhagwati and Srinvasan definitions. Of course, when world prices are fixed, there are no nontraded goods and the value added aggregate and intermediate inputs are used in fixed proportions all of these definitions are the same.

Kreinin, Ramsey, and Kmenta (1971) define two broad types of ERP. The differential form is simply the proportional change in unit value added per proportional change in the tariff structure, while the discrete form is the proportional change in unit value added brought about by the tariff structure. They also note that one might consider the alternative of defining effective tariff rates with respect to variables other than unit value added, and they define various effective rates of protection as the proportional change in total value added, output, labor input, and profits, using Cobb-Douglas and CES functions to provide exact expressions for them.

Finally, Hartigan (1985) has defined the ERP for particular factors or aggregates of factors as the proportional increase in the utilities due to the tariff structure.

For examples of the use of my preferred definition of the ERP, see Gan and Tower (1967) and Loo and Tower (1969). In these papers, the authors provide a table of distortions which afflict the economy in the benchmark equilibrium. These distortions are taxes on nontraded goods and factor incomes, gaps between world and domestic prices of consumer goods (tradable consumption distortions) and effective rates of protection (tradable production distortions). Then they use a computable general equilibrium model to calculate the resource allocation and income distributional effects of perturbing the economy. Finally, they explain the results from the CGE by referring to the distortions, including the ERP as implicit value added subsidy. While the modelling results depend on elasticities as well as the benchmark equilibrium, the ERP as implicit value added subsidy depends only on the benchmark equilibrium. Thus, unlike the GE calculations, it is an objective measure, which does not depend on the modeler's guesses about elasticities, but it helps the consumer of CGE calculations understand what drives them.

Thus, there are many definitions of the ERP in use and one must be careful to define what he means when using the term. To borrow a phrase from David Evans' essay in Grubel and Johnson (1971), perhaps the bottom line is that one should be more concerned with the analysis of the effects of protection than the concept of effective protection in the Bhagwati and Srinvasan senses.

CONCLUSION

To conclude, whereas many like Ethier (1977) have searched for analogies between effective and nominal tariffs, the more appropriate analogy is between the effective tariff and value added subsidy. Perhaps we should even rename the effective tariff the implicit value added subsidy.[18] In fact, Johnson (1971, p. 312), in a chapter which is a reprint of a 1964 lecture, refers to the ERP as "the implicit rate of protection." The problem is that "effective" is defined by Webster as "operative" or "actual," which to me refers to the ultimate consequences of protection after a new general equilibrium has worked itself out, whereas "implicit" is defined as "capable of being understood from something else though unexpressed," which seems to fit the symmetry concept better.

ACKNOWLEDGMENTS

This paper was written while the author was a consultant to the INCA unit of the World Bank, and revised while the author was a visiting professor at Nanjing and Simon Fraser Universities. I am particularly grateful to Garry Pursell and Neil Roger for helping to shape the paper. Thanks for helpful comments also go to Bela Balassa, Trend Bertrand, Max Corden, Sabastian Edwards, Jim Hartigan, Gordon Hughes, Kent Kimbrough and Andrae Maneschi.

NOTES

1. Some authors are inconsistent in their definitions. For example, Johnson (1971, pp. 310, 334) used different definitions which are analogous to Corden's first and second definitions of the NRP, respectively.

2. For discussion of this and related theorems, see Kaempfer and Tower (1982).

3. See, for example, Harry G. Johnson (1965). Gene Grossman has pointed out to me that this theorem also holds in the presence of imperfect competition or multiple imperfect competitors, just as the Lerner Symmetry Theorem does. For the logic of this proposition in the context of the Lerner Symmetry Theorem, see Kaempfer and Tower (1982) and Eaton et al. (1983).

4. See, for example, Corden (1966, 1971). Also, Harberger (1974, p. 75) notes that if intermediate inputs are combined in fixed proportions to produce output, there is an equivalence between any given set of taxes on intermediate inputs and output on the one hand and a tax on value added on the other. The reason that it has not been stated explicitly before is, I believe, that the vast majority of authors have used the definition of the ERP for conceptual purposes which is analogous to Corden's second definition of the NRP, even though in performing calculations they define the ERP as we have defined it.

5. Note that we are pretending here that the value added tax or subsidy is neither charged on imports nor rebated on exports, although countries with value added tax tend to do this in practice. For more on this, see McKinnon (1971).

6. For example, see Ray (1973, p. 256).

7. For example, consider the Metzler paradox which implies that cutting the import tariff may cause the level of imports to fall and domestic output to rise.

8. See, for example, Bertrand (1972), Pursell (1978), and Tower and Pursell (1986, 1987).

9. Proofs of these two propositions are available from the author upon request.

10. Corden (1984) notes that ERPs sometimes take into account consumption taxes and subsidies on inputs as well as production taxes and subsidies. We have defined our ERPs to exclude consumption taxes, but to include subsidies on intermediate inputs, while we have included explicit value added taxation in z but not in ERP. Yet another option would be to include consumption taxes on the good itself in calculating the ERP on production for th home market. Then for each exportable good one would calculate two ERPs, one for home consumption and one for export. If one also incorporated into the ERPs explicit value added taxes and taxes on the use of intermediate inputs, then there would be symmetry between the existing structure of taxes, tariffs, and subsidies, and an alternative consisting of a set of value added subsidies equal to the calculated ERPs combined with taxes on imported consumption goods equal to the difference between consumer prices and world prices.

11. Tower (1984, Chapter 5), finds the procedure to be useful in performing normative analysis. Corden notes that the simple Balassa method (1965) groups nontraded inputs with traded inputs, and treats the former as if they were traded inputs with zero tariffs. He also notes that Balassa has since abandoned use of this method.

12. Balassa and Associates (1982, p. 353) note, however, that "In practice, an approximation can be used instead of the (partial) inversion of the input-output matrix."

13. Bacha and Taylor (1971, p. 202) define the force of x as $1 + x$.

14. The reason that absolute levels of ERPs don't matter is identical to the reason that the level of prices doesn't matter in a simple world where wages and prices are flexible, namely that a proportional increase in the money stock will cause all prices to rise by the same proportion, leaving all relative prices unchanged. However, if there were binding minimum nominal wages, uniformly higher ERPs could raise prices and consequently raise real output levels. Similarly, if there were specific consumption taxes, the inflation generated by uniformly higher ERPs could erode their real value and change real incomes. Finally, international factor mobility will generally invalidate the proposition, for if one country's residents hold wealth denominated in the other country's currency, a uniform increase in domstic ERPs will raise domestic prices and cause domestically owned wealth measured in domestic goods to fall.

However, the proposition also applies even in the presence of international factor mobility and international trade in services, so long as the import or export of factors or services is treated just like the import or export of goods and whatever tariff changes apply to goods apply to them as well. For more on this, see Kaempfer and Tower (1982).

Finally, this equivalence, like all others in this chapter, holds even when factors are not in fixed supply.

15. Corden (1984) and others also note that what matters is nonuniformity in the sale of ERPs. As an aid in understanding the differences between the Corden and Balassa ERPs, note that a system of uniform import tariffs and export subsidies of x percent will result in no rsource misallocation, but crude Corden and sophisticated Corden ERPs for all tradables will be calculated as x percent, while either of the Balassa calculations would yield ERPs of tradable goods of momre than x percent. Similarly, a proportionate increase in the forces of all import tariffs and export subsidies which would have no implications for resource allocation would result in the same proportionate increase in the forces of all crude and sophisticated Corden ERPs for tradables, but that is not true for either of the Balassa measures. This, I think, is a strong indictment of the Balassa methods. Finally, the force of the ERP is sometimes referred to as the ERP coefficient.

16. It should be noted that in applying Balassa's Equations (13) and (14) (p. 354) to calculate NERPs requires that the ERPs with which they are used be calculated as the proportional difference between value added in domestic prices in the post tariff situation and at world prices under free trade, not world prices in the tariff situation. This is because Equations (13) and (14) assume imperfectly elastic foreign excess demands and supplies. However, to calculate ERPs defined with reference to free trade world prices from data applying to the protected equilibrium, when world prices are variable may be a complex process.

17. McKinnon (1971, p. 290) also notes that a value added tax is a better protection device than a tariff since it avoids the consumption distortion. For more on adjustment assistance, see various essayus in Bhagwati (1982).

18. Balassa et al. (1982, p. 17) call the ERP, calculated as the proportional difference in value added at domestic and world prices "the partial equilibrium effective rate."

REFERENCES

Anderson, J. and S. Naya. 1969. Substitution and Two Concepts of Effective Rate of Protection. *American Economic Review* 59: 602-612.

Bacha, E., and L. Taylor. 1971. "Foreign Exchange Shadow Prices: A Critical Review of Current Literature." *Quarterly Journal of Economics* 85:197-224.

Balassa, B. 1965. "Tariff Protection in Industrial Countries: An Evaluation." *Journal of Political Economy* 73: 573-594.

Balssa, B. and Associates. 1971. *The Structure of Protection in Developing Countries*. Baltimore, MD: The Johns Hopkins University Press.

Balassa, B. and Associates. 1982. *Development Strategies in Semi-Industrial Economies.* Baltimore, MD: The Johns Hopkins University Press.

Bertrand, T.J. 1972. "Welfare Indexes with Interindustry Flows: Comment." *Journal of Political Economy* 80: 796-800.

Bhagwati, J.N. and T.N. Srinivasan. 1981. "The Evaluation of Projects at World Prices Under Trade Distortions: Quantitative Restrictions, Monopoly Power in Trade and and Nontraded Goods." *International Economic Review* 22: 385-399.

Bhagwati, J.N. and T.N. Srinivasan. 1983. *Lectures on International Trade.* Cambridge, MA: MIT Press.

Bhagwati, J.N. 1982. *Import Competition and Response.* Chicago, IL: University of Chicago Press.

Corden, W.M. 1966. "The Structure of a Tariff System and the Effective Protective Rate." *Journal of Political Economy* 74: 221-237.

Corden, W.M. 1969. "Effective Protective Rates in the General Equilibrium Model: A Geometric Note." *Oxford Economic Papers* 21: 135-141.

Corden, W.M. 1971. *The Theory of Protection.* Oxford: Clarendon.

Corden, W.M. 1975. "The Costs and Consequences of Protection: A Survey of Empirical Work." In *International Trade and Finance: Frontiers for Research,* ed. P.B. Kenen, 51-91. London: Cambridge University Press.

Corden, W.M. 1984. "The Normative Theory of International Trade." In *Handbook of International Economics,* Vol. 1, ed. R.W. Jones and P.B. Kenen. Amsterdam: North Holland.

Dixit, A. 1985. "Tax Policy in Open Economies." In *Handbook of Public Economics,* ed. A.J. Auerbach and M. Feldstein, 313-374. New York: North-Holland.

Eaton, J., G.M. Grossman, W.H. Kaempfer, and E. Tower. 1983. "The Impact of Monopoly Pricing on the Lerner Symmetry Theorem: A Comment." *Quarterly Journal of Economics* 97: 529-537.

Ethier, W. 1977. "The Theory of Effective Protection in General Equilibrium: Effective Rate Analogues of Nominal Rates." *Canadian Journal of Economics* 10: 233-245.

Gan, K.P., and E. Tower. 1987. "A General Equilibrium Cost-Benefit Approach to Policy Reform and Project Evaluation in Malaysia." *Singapore Economic Review* 32: 46-61.

Grubel, H.G. and H.G. Johnson. 1971. *Effective Tariff Protection.* GATT.

Harberger, A.C. 1974. *Taxation and Welfare.* Chicago: University of Chicago Press.

Harberger, A.C. Undated. "Economic Science and Economic Policy." Manuscript, University of Chicago, Chicago, IL.

Hartigan, J.C. 1985. "Toward a New Definition of the Effective Rate of Protection." *Weltwirtschaftliches Archiv.*

Johnson, H.G. 1965. "The Theory of Tariff Structure with Special Reference to World Trade Development." In *Trade and Development,* eds. H.G. Johnson and P.B. Kenen, 9-29. Libraire Droz.

———. 1971. *Aspects of the Theory of Tariffs.* London: Allen and Unwin.

Kaempfer, W.H., and E. Tower. 1982. "The Balance of Payments Approach to Trade Tax Symmetry Theorems." *Weltwirtschaftliches Archiv* 118: 148-165.

Kreinin, M.E., J.B. Ramsey, and J. Kmenta. 1971. "Factor Substitution and Effective Protection Reconsidered." *American Economic Review* 61: 891-900.

Leith, J.C. 1968. "Sbustitution and Supply Elasticities in Calculating the Effective Protection Rate." *Quarterly Journal of Economics* 82: 588-601.

Little, I.M.D., T. Scitovsky, and M. Scott. 1970. *Industry and Trade in Some Developing Countries.* London: Oxford University Press.

Loo, T., and E. Tower. 1989. "Agricultural Protectionism and the Less Developed Countries: The Relationship between Agricultural Prices, Debt Servicing Capacities and the Need for Development Aid." In Macroeconomic Consequences of Farm Support Policies, ed. A.B. Stoeckel, D. Vincent, and S. Cuthbertson, chapter 2. Durham, NC: Duke University Press.

McKinnon, R.I. 1971. "Protection and the Value Added Tax." In *Effective Tariff Protection,* ed. H.G. Grybel and H.G. Johnson, 287-296. GATT.

Pursell, G. 1978. "Estimating Shadow Exchange Rates: The Ivory Coast." Mimeo, World Bank.

Ray, A. 1973. "Nontraded Inputs and Effective Protection: A General Equilibrium Analysis." *Journal of International Economics* 3: 245-257.

Tower, E. 1984. *The Effective Rate of Protection, Domestic Resource Costs and Shadow Prices: A General Equilibrium Perspective.* World Bank Staff Working Papers, Number 664. Washington, DC: World Bank.

Tower, E., and G. Pursell. 1986. *On Shadow Pricing.* World Bank Staff Working Papers, Number 792. Washington, DC: World Bank.

Tower, E., and G. Pursell. 1987. "On Shadow Pricing Foreign Exchange, Non-Traded Goods and Labor in a Simple General Equilibrium Model." *Oxford Economic Papers* 39: 318-333.

COMMENT ON "ON THE SYMMETRY BETWEEN EFFECTIVE TARIFFS ON VALUE ADDED SUBSIDIES"

Sebastian Edwards

Ed Tower has tried to resuscitate a dead concept, and he has almost succeeded. The concept of effective rate of protection became very popular in the 1960s after the contributions of Corden (1966), Johnson (1965), and Balassa (1965), among others. The main point made by this literature was an important one. In economies where there are intermediate inputs, the structure of nominal protection does not reflect the structure of incentives received by the different sectors. In order to find out the degree of protection actually given to a particular sector (or good), it is necessary to take into account what proportion of the price of the good is represented by unit value added, and what is the tariff applied to the intermediate input. In this way, for example, a good that has a low proportion of domestic value added (say, 20 percent) and whose inputs are subject to a 10 percent tariff will have an effective rate of protection of 50 percent.

From the outset the different contributors to this literature acknowledged that there were a number of conceptual, as well as practical, problems related to the effective rate of protection. A set of papers investigating the effects of introducing many sectors, of incorporating substitution between intermediate inputs, and of allowing for nontraded inputs, proliferated.[1] At the same time a number of studies aimed at computing and comparing effective rates of protection (ERPs), both across time and across countries, were undertaken. In fact, finding a new wrinkle in the effective rate of protection literature became an industry of sorts among graduate students and academics.

In the early literature it was thought that the computation of ERPs would be a useful tool in policy analyses. It was argued that changes in relative ERPs would provide useful information for computing the directions in which resources and sectoral procedures would move, as a result of policy measures (a trade liberalization reform, for example).[2] It was soon discovered, however, that in a general equilibrium setting with more than two goods the ERPs provide no information regarding resource reallocation or changes in income distribution. This finding actually constituted a severe blow to the whole idea of ERPs. Slowly, during the 1970s fewer and fewer papers in international trade addressed the issue, until in the early 1980s a number of authors were quick to proclaim the death of the concept of effective rates of protection.[3] It seems now that the complete dismissal of the concept of ERPs was somewhat premature.

As pointed out by Tower, much of the problems with ERPs were caused by the existence of several definitions. Also, the fact that different authors expected to make different uses of the concept added to the confusion.

Ed Tower is now proposing a very limited—yet practical—use of the ERP concept. He has convincingly argued that ERPs are equivalent to a set of consumption taxes and a set of *subsidies to value added* (of the same rate as the ERPs). Even though this idea was already embodied in earlier discussions on the subject, Tower's clear and convincing exposition is a welcome addition to the literature trying to revive the ERP concept.

Let us say that we agree with the proposition that ERPs provide a good measure of implicit subsidies to value added. What next? Can we make any sensible policy use of this proposition? I would argue that the answer is yes. However, I think that Tower is overstating this case in his discussion of trade liberalization and ERPs (Section XIV). It is true that if in a small country a protective structure is replaced by value-added subsidies of the same rate as the ERPs, neither production nor income distribution will change, However, it is still the case that in a partial equilibrium setting when these equivalent value-added subsidies are reduced, as Tower proposes, we know nothing about the direction in which income distribution and resource allocation will move. And it is presumably the way in which these variables move as the liberalization proceeds that matters to policymakers pursuing this type of reform. In fact, Tower's equivalence proposition doesn't affect in any way the fact that these partial equilibrium type of indicators (i.e., the ERPs or their equivalent value-added subsidies) are unable to tell us anything useful about what will happen once the existing incentive structure is changed.

The paper also has some useful sections where much of the relevant discussions regarding ERP measurement are summarized. In that regard I think that practitioners and policymakers will find the section of ERPs and nontraded inputs useful. Also, the section on the irrelevance of absolute nominal and effective rates of protection is important for policy discussion. Many times policy recommendations are based on the absolute, rather than relative values of tariffs and other incentives. Unfortunately, the paper does not touch on the rather important subject of quotas, ERPs, and equivalent value-added subsidies. A large number of developing countries have based their commercial policies on the extensive use of quantitative restrictions. It has been well established in the literature that there are many circumstances under which quotas and nominal tariffs are not equivalent. It would be interesting, then, to see an extension of Tower's discussion to the case on "nonequivalent" quotas.

To sum up, Ed Tower has provided us with an interesting paper that aims at partially resuscitating the concept of effective rate of protection. In order to do this he starts by discussing the alternative definitions of ERP used in the literature. He then settles for a useful, quite unambitious definition according to which the effect of an ERP on production is equivalent to the effect of a subsidy on value-added of the same rate. It is important to realize that, while this definition is based on a correct equivalence theorem, it has a somewhat limited practical or policy use. It is still true that in a general equilibrium setting with many goods we don't know how the manipulation of the ERPs, or their equivalent value-added subsidies, will affect the direction of resource movements or of changes in income distribution. Tower has been somewhat successful in resuscitating the ERP concept. However, in their new incarnation ERPs are only marginally more useful than before.

NOTES

1. Good coverages of the topics discussed in the 1960s are provided in Corden (1971) and Johnson (1971).
2. See, for example, Johnson (1969).
3. Most modern textbooks either ignore ERPs or caution students about their use. See, for example, Kenen (1985). In the recently published *Handbook of International Economics,* most authors that cover the subject point out the deficiencies of ERP.

REFERENCES

Balassa, Bala. 1965. "Tariff Protection in Industrial Countries: An Evaluation." *Journal of Political Economy.*

Corden, Max. 1966. "The Structure of a Tariff System and the Effective Protective Rate." *Journal of Political Economy.*

Corden, Max. 1971. *The Theory of Protection.* Oxford: Clarendon Press.

Johnson, Harry G. 1965. "The Theory of Tariff Structure with Special Reference to World Trade and Development." *Trade and Development,* ed. H.G. Johnson and P.B. Kenen. Geneva: Librerie Droz.

Johnson, Harry G. 1969. "The Theory of Effective Protection and Preferences." *Economica.*

Johnson, Harry G. 1971. *Aspects of the Theory of Tariffs.* London: George Allen and Unwin.

Kenen, Peter B. 1985. *The International Economy.* Englewood Cliffs, NJ: Prentice-Hall.

ON THE VALIDITY OF THE LERNER NEUTRALITY AND SYMMETRY THEOREMS IN THE PRESENCE OF NONTRADED GOODS

Victor Canto, William H. Kaempfer,
and Edward Tower

INTRODUCTION

The title of this volume, *Industrial Policy and International Trade*, raises the question: What is the single most important message that an international economist has to offer about industrial policy? Two messages come to our minds.

One is that any attempt to subsidize all domestic sectors by a system of uniform import tariffs and export subsidies is bound to have no effect on the domestic economy, simply because under a flexible exchange rate it will set up an incipient balance of trade surplus which will appreciate the domestic currency by just enough to completely neutralized the initial impact of the tax subsidy scheme, while under a fixed exchange rate it will generate a balance of trade surplus, which via the Hume mechanism will raise domestic wages and prices of other nontraded goods and nontraded inputs to such a level that the initial stimulus to output will be completely eradicated in each and every sector. Thus all we are left with is the extra costs associated with running an administrative machinery to implement the tax subsidy program, and the resources used up in smuggling imports, overinvoicing exports, and policing these illegal activities.[1] Since this combination of import tariffs, export subsidies, and either inflation or exchange rate change is neutral with respect to resource allocation (except for the effects noted above) we refer to this idea as the Lerner Neutrality Theorem.

The second message is that whenever we use a uniform import tariff to protect our import competing sectors, we implicitly tax exports, which will generally mean that resources will flow out of the export sectors into the import competing ones.[2] Here, the mechanism is that an import tariff under flexible exchange rates sets up an incipient balance of trade surplus which appreciates the currency and makes it harder to sell exports, and under fixed exchange rates it sets up, via the Hume mechanism, a monetary expansion which causes inflation and thereby squeezes exports. Similarly, an export tax also implicitly taxes imports. Intuitively, the idea is that if some adjustment mechanism keeps the trade balance in equilibrium any policy that shrinks the value of imports must simultaneously shrink the value of exports, so that any policy which affects imports must also affect exports. The idea that an import tariff and an export tariff of *x* percent have identical impacts on all real variables is known as the Lerner Symmetry theorem. It is a particularly succinct way of stating that protection creates losers as well as gainers.

Kaempfer and Tower (1982) show that the Lerner Neutrality and Symmetry Theorems hold under quite a wide range of circumstances. Among other things, they show that the theorems hold in the presence of nontraded goods, but because they try to be general, their proofs are somewhat formidable. McDougall (1970) also shows that the Symmetry Theorem holds in the presence of nontraded goods, but his proof is difficult to grasp. To highlight the intuition behind these ideas, we offer in this paper simpler and more accessible proofs for a special case.

THE NEUTRALITY THEOREM

Let our economy's trading equilibrium be defined by the following fourteen-equation model:

$$X_i = X_i(P_i/W) \qquad i = 1,2 \tag{1,2}$$

$$C_i = C_i\,(P_1/W, P_2/W, M/W, R/W) \qquad i = 1,2 \tag{3,4}$$

$$\ell = \ell(P_1/W, P_2/W, M/W, R/W) \tag{5}$$

$$X_i - C_i = F_i(P_1^*, P_2^*) \tag{6,7}$$

$$\sum_i P_i^*\,[X_i - C_i] = 0 \tag{8}$$

$$L_1 + L_2 + \ell = \bar{L} \tag{9}$$

$$L_i = L_i(X_i) \qquad i = 1,2 \tag{10, 11}$$

$$P_i = e(1+t)P_i^* \qquad i = 1,2 \tag{12, 13}$$

$$R = 0 \tag{14}$$

where domestic variables are starless and foreign ones are starred.

X_i = output of good i,
P_i = the domestic price of good i (in U.S. dollars, i.e., domestic currency)
W = wage rate (in U.S. dollars),
C_i = consumption of good i,
M = money stock (in U.S. dollars),
R = net revenue from trade taxes and subsidies,
ℓ = leisure,
P_i^* = the world price of good i (in £, i.e., foreign currency),
L_i = labor employed in the production of good i,
L = the fixed labor endowment,
e = the price of foreign exchange (in \$/£), and
t = the common import tariff or export subsidy on all traded goods expressed as a fraction of the world price.

The equations are interpreted as follows:

Equations (1, 2). Good i is produced using sector-specific capital, which is in fixed supply, plus labor. Thus its output depends on its price relative to the wage rate.

Equations (3, 4) and (5). The consumption of each good and leisure depends on the prices of the two goods relative to the wage rate, net revenue from trade taxes (which is assumed to be redistributed to the private sector), and the quantity of money measured in units of labor.

Equations (6, 7). The world prices of the two traded goods depend on domestic net exports of the two traded goods.

Equation (8). The flexibility of domestic prices and wages and either the exchange rate or the money stock, along with zero international capital mobility, assures trade balance equilibrium.

Equation (9). The labor endowment is allocated among productive uses and leisure.

Equations (10, 11). Each sector's labor use depends on its output.

Equations (12, 13). The domestic prices of the two traded goods are equal to their world prices multiplied by the price of foreign exchange multiplied by one plus the common import tariff cum export subsidy expressed as a proportion of world prices.

Equation (14). Trade balance, combined with the common import tariff cum export subsidy, assures that the government collects zero net revenues from its tax subsidy scheme.

Our fourteen equation system cam be solved for the fourteen endogenous variables, which are X_l, P_i, C_i, P_i^*, L_i, $(i = 1, 2)$, $\underline{R}$, W, ℓ, and e, in terms of the exogenous variables which are t, $\bar{L}$ and M. Thus, it is conceptually straightforward to differentiate the entire system and solve for the impacts of changes in the exogenous variables on all of the endogenous variables.

The Lerner Neutrality Theorem can be said to hold if a change in t affects no real variables. To find whether this is the case, note that e and t enter the system only as $e(1 + t)$, the effective exchange rate. Thus $e(1 + t)$ can be treated as a single endogenous variable. This means that if we have already solved the system for e given some value of t, and we change the value of t, and simultaneously adjust e so that $e(1 + t)$ is unchanged, the system will continue to be in equilibrium at the initial values of all our endogenous variables except for e (which is only a nominal variable). Thus, the point is that the exchange rate authority can pick an exchange rate that will neutralize any import tax cum export subsidy.

Looking at the problem in another way, we can treat $(1 + t)e$ as a single endogenous variable, which is to say that, as t changes, under a flexible exchange rate e will automatically adjust to leave $(1 + t)e$ unchanged, along with all of the other endogenous variables. Thus, we have proven that the Lerner Neutrality Theorem continues to hold even in the presence of nontraded goods.

Alternatively, if we were to fix the exchange rate permanently and to let the money stock vary, then if the system is initially in equilibrium with free trade, when the tax subsidy rises to t, the system will continue to be in equilibrium when all nominal variables except the exchange rate (P_i, W, M and R) are also increased by a proportion t, thereby leaving all relative prices and real variables unchanged.

In this proof, as in the one to follow, we have not addressed the problem of multiple equilibria. All we are saying is that to each equilibrium in the initial situation there corresponds an equilibrium in the second situation which is identical in all real respects.

This neutrality in the presence of nontraded goods implies that a nondistortionary intervention in the traded sector will also be nondistorting of allocation decisions over nontraded goods. Furthermore, for an existing, distorting trade policy, there is an offsetting package of interventions to correct the distortion. Thus, if a nation with a system of import substitution inducing tariffs embarks on a program of export subsidization, the level of distortion in the economy will fall, even with nontraded goods.

The neutrality of the trade intervention package, however, does not diminish the possibility of directly unproductive activity like smuggling, evasive activity like over- or underinvoicing and enforcement costs. Thus, while two interventions may appear to neutralize each other, in fact they both create costs that are absent in the otherwise symmetric state of free trade.

III. THE SYMMETRY THEOREM

The Lerner Symmetry Theorem states that, when an import tariff is replaced by an export tariff of the same magnitude, no real variables will alter.

To prove this proposition we use substantially the same model as before, but with certain changes. We replace Equations (12) and (13) with:

$$P_1 = e\,[1 + t\,(1 - \delta)]\,O_1^* \tag{15}$$

$$O_2\,(1 + t\,\delta) = eP_2^* \tag{16}$$

and

$$e = (1 + t\delta)e_0 \tag{17}$$

where δ is a dummy variable that takes on a value of 0 in period 0 and 1 in period 1, which is to say in period 0 there is an import tariff levied at a fraction t on imported good 1, no tariff on exported good 2, and the exchange rate equals e_o. Then in period 1, $\delta = 1$, which is to say the import tariff is replaced by an export tariff equal to a fraction t of the sellers' price, and simultaneously the price of foreign currency is raised by a fraction t. These equations can be recombined as:

$$P_1 = e_0\,(1 + t\delta)\,[1 + t(1 - \delta)]P_1^* \tag{12'}$$

and

$$P_2 = e_0P_2^* \tag{13'}$$

Similarly, equation 14 is replaced by an alternative. Net revenue from trade taxes can be written as:

$$R = \sum_i (P_i - eP^*_i)\,[C_i - X_i] \tag{18}$$

Our postulated trade balance equilibrium causes this to be replaced by:

$$R = \sum_i P_i[C_i - X_i] \tag{19}$$

which invoking (12') and (13') can be rewritten as:

$$R = e_0\,\{[1 + t\delta]\,[1 + t(1 - \delta)]P^*_1\,(C_1 - X_1) + P^*_2[C_2 - X_2]\} \tag{14'}$$

Equations (1)-(11) and (12′)-(14′) can be solved for Equation (14)'s endogenous variables, which are the same as before except that e has been replaced by e_0. Note that, since our equation system is identical whether $\delta = 0$ or $\delta = 1$, any solution which obtains for period 0 also obtains for period 1. Thus, replacing our import tariff with an export tariff at the same rate and appreciating the foreign currency by that same proportion leaves all real and nominal variables except the exchange rate unchanged and our theorem proven.

Alternatively, we could have left the exchange rate fixed permanently and cut the money stock and all nominal variables by the same proportion. In that case all domestic nominal variables (P_i, W, and M) would have had to have fallen by the same proportion to restore the same real equilibrium, but at that equilibrium relative prices and real quantities would have been preserved at their initial levels.

IV. POSTSCRIPT

Two quotes from the Old Masters may help to put the issue of international trade and industrial policy into perspective.

Perhaps it is appropriate to recall Edgeworth's (1908, pp. 555-556) commentary on Bickerdike's analysis of the optimum tariff, and for "optimum tariff" substitute "protection as industrial policy," and for Mr. Bickerdike your favorite advocate of discretionary industrial policy.

> Thus the direct use of the theory is likely to be small. But it is to be feared that its abuse will be considerable. It affords to unscrupulous advocates of vulgar Protection a particularly specious pretext for introducing the thin edge of the fiscal wedge. Mr. Bickerdike may be compared to a scientist who, by a new analysis, has discovered that strychnine may be administered in small doses with prospect of advantage in one or two more cases than was previously known; the result of this discovery may be to render the drug more easily procurable by those whose intention, or at least whose practice is not medicinal.... Let us admire the skill of the analyst, but label the subject of his investigation POISON.

All in all, it seems to us that the most appropriate industrial policy is to treat all tradable goods equally and in an administratively efficient fashion. In these regards, selecting the appropriate exchange rate and combining it with free trade dominates attempts to pick the optimum basket of explicit import restrictions and export bounties.

Our second quote is from Sir Nathaniel Brent's (1645) discussion of trade and monopoly. He writes:

> [The granting of monopoly power to trade] hath bin like an Ulcer upon the Body politique of this Kingdome a long time, which hath been often rub'd and lanc'd, yet it clos'd againe and gatherd more corruption than formerly, and now requires a greater cure than ever (pp. A1-A2).
>
> Trade (though the comparison be homely) is like Dung, which being close kept in a heap or two stinks, but being spread abroad, it doth fertilize the earth and make it fructify.... (p. 25)

While we are not sure how much further we would wish to carry this analogy, it does seem that free trade is a very effective antitrust policy and that any interference with it under the guise of industrial policy, mercantilism, or taxing foreigners will weaken its antimonopoly impact.

ACKNOWLEDGMENT

The authors are grateful to Kiyoun Han for helpful comments.

NOTES

1. These "collection" costs of trade policy are typically overlooked. However, as Corden (1974, p. 65) notes, "One cannot excuse a failure to stress their importance." Also, see Haberler (1967), who argues that import taxes combined with export subsidies are in fact a very subsitute for the realignment of exchange rates.
2. We need the "generally" here to accommodate the Metzler paradox.

REFERENCES

Brent, Sir Nathaniel. 1972. "A Discourse Consisting of Motives for the Enlargement and Freedom of Trade." In *Mercantilist Views on Trade and Monopoly,* ed. Leonard Silk. New York: Arno.

Corden, W.M. 1974. *Trade Policy and Economic Welfare.* Oxford: Oxford University Press.

Edgeworth, Frank Y. 1908. "Appreciations of Mathematical Theories." *Economic Journal*: 541-556.

Haberler, Gottfried. 1967. "Import Taxes and Export Subsidies as a Substitute for the Realignment of Exchange Rates." *Kyklos* 20: 17-23.

Kaempfer, W.H., and E. Tower. 1982. "The Balance of Payments Approach to Trade Tax Symmetry Theorems." *Weltwirtschaftliches Archiv,* Band 118, Heft 1.

McDougall, I.A. 1970. "Non-Traded Commodities and The Pure Theory of International Trade." In *Studies in International Economics,* ed. I.A. McDougall and R.H. Snape, ch. 10. Amsterdam: North Holland.

JAPANESE HIGH TECHNOLOGY, GOVERNMENT POLICY, AND EVOLVING COMPARATIVE ADVANTAGE IN GOODS AND SERVICES

Gary R. Saxonhouse

INDUSTRIAL POLICY AND CAPITAL MARKETS

American policymakers wish to know whether resource allocation in Japan, as between advancing and declining industries and as between imparting highly sophisticated technical training and less sophisticated training, is in the some sense superior to what is observed in the United States. The basic textbooks in economics assure us that both engineers and economists have something important to say about questions of this kind. As is well known, what economists have to say runs along two fairly well-trodden paths. In comparing the Japanese experience with the American experience, evidence of market distortion and market failure must be examined.

Table 1. 1973 Net Tax/Subsidy Rates for the United States, Japan, and the United Kingdom by SITC Sector

	United States Factor Taxes		*Japan Factor Taxes*		*United Kingdom Factor Taxes*	
	Capital	*Labor*	*Capital*	*Labor*	*Capital*	*Labor*
Traded Goods						
(1) Agr., for., & fish	9.0%	7.0%	23.6%	3.7%	6.4%	8.2%
(310) Food, bev.	178.2	11.0	86.8	9.1	183.4	9.8
(321) Textiles	138.9	13.1	35.4	9.9	121.4	11.5
(322) Wearing apparel	138.9	13.1	35.4	8.1	240.2	11.1
(323) Leather products	138.9	13.1	35.4	9.4	276.5	12.8
(324) Footwear	138.9	13.1	35.4	9.4	276.5	12.8
(331) Wood products	49.6	12.5	38.4	10.5	116.6	7.9
(332) Furn. & fixt.	49.6	12.5	38.4	10.5	116.6	7.9
(341) Paper & paper prod.	96.8	10.3	38.4	9.6	96.9	8.7
(35A) Paper & paper prod.	96.8	10.3	38.4	9.6	96.9	8.7
(35B) Petrol & rel. prod.	19.7	8.4	41.9	11.9	230.6	12.0
(355) Rubber products	144.7	10.5	41.9	9.0	120.3	9.2
(36A) Nonmet. misc. prod.	81.0	10.3	40.2	9.8	120.3	9.2
(362) Glass & glass prod.	81.0	10.3	40.2	9.8	120.3	9.2
(371) Iron & steel	81.0	10.3	37.8	11.0	6.3	9.8
(372) Nonferr. met.	81.0	10.3	34.7	11.5	6.3	9.8
(381) Metal prod.	81.0	10.3	45.0	9.9	6.3	9.8
(382) Nonelec. mach.	103.5	10.5	38.9	9.6	390.2	9.0
(383) Elec. mach.	103.5	10.5	38.9	9.6	390.2	9.0
(384) Transp. equip.	86.8	9.6	44.1	9.9	282.5	8.2
(38A) Misc. Manu.	86.6	10.5	43.2	9.4	144.1	9.1
Nontraded Goods						
(2) Mining & quarrying	34.3	9.6	50.1	19.0	-55.9	9.7
(4) Elec., gas. & water	45.7	2.6	22.8	16.2	-7.2	8.1
(5) Construction	133.3	10.4	39.3	10.7	43.9	9.2
(6) Whole. & ret. trade	112.0	10.5	29.9	8.7	275.5	9.7
(7) Tr., stor., & comm.	186.6	11.8	37.4	10.3	-47.4	7.3
(8) Fin., ins., & real est.	135.2	9.7	41.5	11.0	144.9	6.5
(9) Comm., soc., & pers. ser.	21.2	9.6	27.9	8.5	42.9	12.9

Source: See R. Stern and A. Deardorff, "The Effects of Domestic Tax Subsidies and Import Tariffs on the Structure of Production in the United States, United Kingdom and Japan," in *Proceedings of Sixth Annual Conference,* International Economic Study Group, University of Sussex, Rōdōshō, Tōkei kyoku, Jōhōbu, *Fukuri hassei shisetsu tō rōdō hiyō no jitai*; Okurashō, hōjōkin benron, Nohon ginko, Tōkei hyoku, *Omō kigyō keiei bunseki*; Sōrifu, Tōkei kyoku, Chōsa bu, Kōjin kigyō chōsa nenpō.

Market Distortion

The most obvious source of market distortion in Japan, as in the United States and elsewhere, results from government intervention of one sort or another. To the extent that government intervention in resource allocation is primarily through sectoral tax and subsidy policy, Table 1, which presents sectoral effective tax rates in the early 1970s net of subsidies for Japan, the United States, and the United Kingdom, is particularly instructive. The coefficient of variation in effective capital tax rates and in the ratio of effective capital tax rates to effective labor tax rates is substantially lower in Japan than in the United States and the United Kingdom. Moreover, the mean of the sectoral ratios of effective capital tax rates to effective labor tax rates is lower in Japan than in the United States and the United Kingdom. A straightforward interpretation of this table suggests that, in this dimension of industrial policy, the Japanese government, rather than picking winners and losers among sectors, acted to remove intersectoral distortions, while generally subsidizing capital relative to labor. Another alternative interpretation, first put forward by Ryutarō Komiya, has argued that the Japanese government was under political pressure to help, on an ad hoc basis, so many of Japan's industrial sectors, that its industrial policy wound up helping no particular sector at all![1] Under either interpretation the net impact of government intervention through tax subsidy policy in Japan appears small. By contrast, in the United States and the United Kingdom, sectoral intervention by the government, while not necessarily pursued under a comprehensive framework, also does not appear to wash out.

Market Failure

Despite the founding of the Tokyo Stock Exchange as early as 1878, until quite recently capital markets remained underdeveloped in Japan. Traditionally, most capital has been rationed by the Japanese banking system. The emergence of large industrial groups in Japan, long in advance of American conglomerates, must be attributed to the concentration of capital in Japan. The traditional dominant role of a small number of Japanese banks in capital allocation, and the traditionally close regulation of these banks by the Japanese government, has surely been more significant than differential taxes and direct subsidies as a mechanism of industrial policy in Japan. This government bank group interaction on capital allocation, however, can be thought of as nothing more than an attempt to simulate market processes. What effective elements of industrial policy exist in Japan can be interpreted as an effort to overcome the distortions which might result from the long-time absence of well-developed capital markets.

If Japanese industrial policy has been a substitute for capital markets, which only became significant in Japanese resource allocation in the 1980s, why is a Japanese-style industrial policy being urged for economies which have had well-developed capital markets for decades?[2] Doubtless some advocates of Japanese-style industrial policy mistakenly believe that Japanese governmental agencies are creating large, socially benign sectoral differentials in effective tax subsidy rates. Many other advocates, however, just doubt the ability of capital markets to allocate scarce resources efficiently.

What is wrong with capital markets? This is not a place to review the at least ninety-years-old plan versus market literature, which includes much of the substance of modern day microeconomics, or to evaluate security and finance regulation in the United States.[3] Rather, the analysis here will simply discuss Japanese inspired criticism of American performance.[4] Such criticisms complain that American corporate managers are excessively short sighted in their decision making because of American corporations' overly heavy reliance on equity markets. Decisions are allegedly made with undue concern about how any given action will affect the next quarterly earnings statement.

To be sure, reliance on equity financing has led to compensation packages for top-level American managers where large bonus payments are tied to the market performance of company equities.[5] This, however, need not lead to an excessively short-run outlook for corporate managers. Tying compensation to equity market evaluation rather than directly to earnings should help the longer term view to prevail. Efficiently working equity markets should distinguish between ephemeral manipulation and long-term structural improvements. Only if it is accepted that there is pervasive and persistent destabilizing speculation is it possible to argue that a program of regular preoccupation with quarterly earning reports by top management could not make sense.

In point of fact, the Japanese mistrust of equity financing, which has very nearly taken on the status of an issue in the bilateral economic diplomacy between Japan and the United States, is rooted in the experience of many Japanese business leaders during the pre-Pacific War period with equity financing and may have little to do with current conditions in the United States. In prewar Japan, new investment was commonly equity financed. Equities were characteristically pledged by owners as collateral for the bank loan which permitted their purchase. The interests of equity holders, which dominated the prewar boards of directors of Japanese enterprises, demanded that high dividends be paid out so that equity holder bank loans might be serviced. The long-term interests of the firm were regularly sacrificed to the liquidity needs of the dominant equity holders.

Quite apart from avoiding the consequences of destabilizing speculation, does Japanese government-business interaction, which is Japanese industrial policy, deal successfully with market failure? New industrial activities involve learning and other pioneering activity the social benefit of which cannot necessarily be internalized. Presumably a successfully functioning industrial policy should bridge the gap between social and private benefits and social and private costs. If such externalities are large, reliance on capital markets to allocate resources will lead to inferior outcomes.

Are such externalities large? Of course, opinions on this question vary widely, but the economic growth accounting literature does provide one approach to an economy-wide assessment of this issue. Economic growth accounting, if properly done, should distinguish between the role of primary inputs (such as labor), the role of produced inputs (such as capital and some qualitative improvements in labor), and the presence of externalities, including risk for which there is no social insurance.[6] If government policy has intervened such that marginal social benefits equal marginal social cost, then in the absence of scale economies or diseconomies, and assuming that all relevant inputs and outputs have been properly measured and included in the construction of the indexes, the rate of growth of the aggregate output index should equal the rate of growth of the aggregate input index. Table 2 presents the results of a number of major studies of Japanese postwar economic growth. If the success of industrial policy is marked by the absence of large measured total factor productivity change, then Table 2, while admittedly imperfect evidence, does suggest a failure of Japanese industrial policy.

An alternative perspective on the consequences of Japanese industrial policy might be gained by examining the evolution of Japanese comparative advantage, and therefore Japanese industrial structure, in a cross-national empirical framework. If Japanese experience is properly normalized for Japan's capital stock, labor force, geographic position, and material resource endowment, is there any variance left in the Japanese experience from that of other major industrialized economies that might be explained by an efficacious Japanese industrial policy?

As described in the Appendix and following Chenery's work, it is possible to develop standards for normal export and import patterns by empirically implementing cross-nationally a version of the Heckscher-Ohlin Theory of Comparative Advantage.[7] Unlike Chenery's work, and appropriate to a consideration of Japan's special position, this work involves an extensive treatment of the role of natural resources and the differing qualities of factor inputs. By drawing directly on modern production theory it is possible to obtain an explicit functional form within which the Heckscher-Ohlin framework can be implemented.[8] This general equilibrium trade framework in turn allows a multiplicative errors in variables specification which permits the estimation of national quality of factor inputs differentials as a byproduct of the estimation of the entire analytical framework. Using these procedures on cross-national data for the period prior to 1973, it is found that there is nothing abnormal about Japanese trade and industrial patterns. Japanese behavior can be explained within the context of a framework common to most other participants in the

Table 2. Sources of Japanese Economic Growth by Author/Date (in percent)

	Kanamori		*Denison-Chung*		*Watanabe*		*Ohkawa*		*Hulton-Nishimizu*	
	1955-1968	*Percent of Real Product Growth Explained*	*1953-1971*	*Percent of Real Product Growth Explained*	*1952-1964*	*Percent of Real Product Growth Explained*	*1955-1961*	*Percent of Real Product Growth Explained*	*1955-1971*	*Percent of Real Product Growth Explained*
Real Product	10.1		8.77		9.6		13.04		11.45	
Growth Explained by Real Capital Input Growth	2.72	26.9	2.10	23.9	3.4	35.4	2.82	21.6	6.68	58.3
Real Labor Input Growth	1.31	13.0	1.85	21.1	1.1	11.5	3.46	26.5	1.89	16.5
Employment	1.03	10.2	1.14	13.0	0.9	9.4	—	—	1.69	16.5
Hours	-0.07	-0.7	0.21	2.4	0.06	0.6	—	—	0.03	0.3
Quality (age)	0.21	2.1	0.14	1.6	0.02	0.2	—	—	0.22	1.9
Education	0.14	1.4	0.34	3.9	0.12	1.3	—	—	—	—
Total Factor Productivity Change	6.1	61.0	4.82	55.0	5.1	53.1	6.75	51.8	2.88	25.2

Sources: H. Kanamori, "What Makes the Japanese Economic Growth Rate?" *Japanese Economic Studies* (Summer 1972): 31-48; E.F. Denison and W.K. Chung, *How Japan's Economy Grew So Fast* (Washington, DC: Brookings Institution, 1976); T. Watanabe, "Improvement of Labor Quality and Economic Growth: Japan's Post-War Experience," *Economic Development and Cultural Change* (April 1974); K. Ohkawa, "Nihon keizai no seisan to bumpai, 1905-63," *Keizai kenkya* (1968); C.R. Hulten and M. Nishimizu, "The Sources of Japan Economic Growth, 1955-71," *Review of Economics and Statistics* (November 1978).

world economy and without particular reference to distinctive Japanese policies.

INDUSTRIAL POLICY, SCIENCE AND TECHNOLOGY POLICY, AND LABOR MARKETS

The foregoing analysis suggests that Japanese industrial policy has been a substitute, not a complement, for the market allocation of capital. While there is no evidence to suggest that such policies have been worse than the market allocation of capital, neither is there compelling evidence to suggest they have been superior. A similar analysis of Japanese industrial policy can be done from the perspective of the labor market.

With the abolition of slavery, and even in its presence, modern industrialized economies face the difficult problem of encouraging socially optimal accumulation of skills. Until the postwar period, there were few alternatives to self- or family financing of the acquisition of new skills. Whether training was acquired in a firm or in an educational institution, the trainees or students had to acquire the financing on their own. With worker mobility, firms providing training in general skills had little incentive not to implicitly charge their workers for this service. At the same time, because skills, then as now, were embodied in individuals and there was no tangible collateral that could be confiscated for nonpayment of loans, it was difficult to seek financing for skill accumulation from financial intermediaries. In consequence, in both prewar Japan and the United States, with skill accumulation heavily dependent on personal or family resources, there was probably a persistent underaccumulation of socially beneficial skills.[9]

In the postwar period, increasingly complex industrial life has been facilitated by, and has demanded, a more rapid accumulation of industrial skills. In the United States, from the beginning of the postwar period, there have been a number of extremely significant programs to either directly subsidize skill accumulation or to facilitate the use of financial intermediaries to finance such accumulation. These programs, which include Veterans

Educational Benefits, which began in the immediate postwar period with the G.I. Bill of Rights, and Guaranteed Student Loans, almost all require that training be done in educational institutions that are in some fashion or other accredited. These programs have helped to greatly increase the demand for, and therefore, in time, the supply of, vocational undergraduate and graduate education in the United States.

In Japan, in the postwar period, skill accumulation has been institutionalized in a very different way. There have been no major government programs directly subsidizing individual education. There has been a relatively modest increase in the number of heavily subsidized public institutions that provide education at a very low tuition, but for the most part, the very large increase in the number of Japanese receiving higher education has been at private universities which until the last fifteen years financed themselves almost entirely out of tuition charges.[10]

In the absence of large direct grants on the American scale from the government and facing an unsubsidized student body, most Japanese universities have not developed extensive research programs, particularly in the sciences and engineering, and have made little effort to offer, much less to excel, in specialized graduate training programs. Rather, in Japan, training has become much more the function of the firm. To a far greater extent than was characteristic during the prewar period, this training has been paid for by the firm within the context of a permanent employment program.[11]

Japanese permanent employment programs, which are prevalent in the larger Japanese firms and which include perhaps one-third of the total Japanese male manufacturing labor force, make it economically feasible for a firm's labor force to be optimally trained at firm expense. Large Japanese firms operating under permanent employment programs pay their workers in large measure in accordance with the number of years they have been employed by the firm.[12] In consequence, Japanese workers have strong incentives not to voluntarily leave the firm for which they are working. At the same time, by having the option of being able to pay their workers less than their marginal productivity without these workers leaving the firm, it is possible for the firm to recoup whatever explicit and implicit training outlays are in the firm's interest to make.

Quite like the case of capital markets and industrial policy, at one level Japan's permanent employment system can be viewed as a substitute for a fully developed vocational and higher educational system. Unlike the capital markets-industrial policy case, however, there is some reason to believe that the outcomes of these differing means of skill accumulation really are somewhat different.

In the United States, because training outside the firm is subsidized relative to training within the firm, and because a disproportionate amount of training does take place outside firms, Americans are more generally and more theoretically trained than their Japanese counterparts. Prior to their entry into a firm, a significant proportion of the American labor force acquires an occupation or professional identification which will remain a significant determinant of their compensation during their working life. Indeed, since an American firm will have little incentive to provide, without cost, anything other than training in extremely firm-specific skills, American work experience may well serve to reinforce this identification.

By contrast, in Japan, where much of the work force lacks significant incentive to acquire extra firm-advanced training, a far larger proportion of total training will be done within the firm and this training will in all likelihood by (1) less general, and less theoretical and systematic, than might be received in extra-firm educational institutions in the United States, and (2) more closely coordinated with the Japanese firms' actual needs.[13] Because of the less general and theoretical character of the training, because retraining as well as training costs can be recouped by the firm, and finally because a Japanese firm's personnel has little incentive to use a professional or occupational association as a lever to job mobility, there will be a relative lack of professional and occupational orientation and identification.[14] This lack of professional orientation, which extends to a firm's technical, scientific, and managerial personnel, will have a number of important consequences for Japanese firms and government behavior relative to what is common in the United States. Most important here, this relative lack of professional orientation will make less likely those informal associations of professionals across firms which encourage the nonmarket transfer of economically useful information.

There is no better way to document the relative leakage of economically useful information than to compare the modus operandi of American and Japanese research and development (R&D) facilities. Each day in an American facility considerable time is spent describing and documenting precisely what has been attempted and what has been accomplished by each member of an R&D team. This documentation goes far beyond what is necessary for scientific and technological replication, and is done with an eye to potential litigation if and when proprietary scientific information leaks. As might be predicted, there is almost no documentation done for this purpose in Japan.[15]

In some regard, the relatively small amount of leakage of proprietary information among Japanese firms is highly desirable. In the United States, notwithstanding a vast legal effort to protect the proprietary fruits of very expensive R&D, there is a great deal of slippage. The continuing storm of litigation in California's Silicon Valley is certainly proof of this. In consequence, the rate of return to research and development, everything else being equal, is less, and less resources are committed to this end than might be socially desirable.

The preceding point of view assumes, however, that interchange is always among unequals. Firms investing in the production of new information are always exploited by firms wishing to be free riders. An alternative perspective might emphasize informal interchange among equals. More positively, leakage of proprietary information might be called technological diffusion. Professionally oriented, potentially mobile managers and technical personnel might be implicitly disclosing proprietary information in order to enhance their employment prospects at some later date, but they also might be disclosing such information in order to receive in exchange, albeit informally, proprietary information of commensurate value. Such trading of information could, of course, make everyone better off. And such information swapping can be quite complementary to explicit market transactions in information. Actually, in many instances, such informal trading will be a necessary prerequisite to more formal market transactions.

To the extent that such informal exchanges are useful, and to the extent that they are facilitated by having professionally oriented technical and managerial personnel, it is quite possible that Japan, by virtue of its employment system, does have a competitive handicap. Here again the Japanese government steps forward to accomplish deliberately what is done informally by market forces in the United States. One of the major presumptive benefits of Japan's explicit industrial policy is the detailed sectoral planning which it requires. This planning, which is traditionally done at the bureau level in the Ministry of International Trade and Industry, requires the intimate participation of the representative of individual firms with relevant government officials. This very process necessitates a more formal information sharing and provides the basis for associations which might encourage more informal sharing.

More narrowly, the Japanese government's widely discussed interfirm cooperative research programs are an effort to insure that Japanese R&D efforts do not become, by virtue of Japan's permanent employment system, still more narrowly firm-specific than is true in the United States. Once again, another element of Japanese industrial policy can be seen as a substitute for, not a complement to, American style practices.

That cooperation among firms in Japan does not come easily may be illustrated by the experience with research on Very Large Scale Integration (VLSI) electronic chips. This project was initiated in 1975 as part of a continuing effort by the Japanese government to direct and promote the Japanese computer industry. The Machinery and Information Services Bureau of the Ministry of International Trade and Industry encouraged Nippon Electric (NEC), Toshiba, Hitachi, Fujitsu, and Mitsubishi Electric (MELCO) to establish the VLSI Technology Research Association which in turn established a joint research laboratory at Kawasaki.[16] The carrot for participation in this research association, over and above the usual 100 percent first year write-off of all fixed assets used in research association activities was $130 million in direct government subsidies spread out over four years.

Despite the maintenance of a joint research laboratory, which is virtually unique for a research association, each VLSI project handled within the laboratory was separately conducted by teams of researchers drawn almost entirely from a single company.[17] Each project team designed their machinery and then had it built by their own firm using a separate part of the Kawasaki laboratory. There was only irregular contact between the various project teams. Each firm participating in the VLSI Research Association brought their own technology to the project and took back to their firms further advances on company-specific information.[18] Of the more than 1,000 patents developed by the joint laboratory at Kawasaki, only 50 were held jointly or individually by the Japanese government.

It is highly significant that Nippon Telephone and Telegraph (NTT), a company which maintains an extremely strong technology for making electronic chips, chose not to directly participate in the MITI-sponsored research association. The Post Office, which owns half of NTT, has been able to protect it from MITI interference.[19] NTT has been careful to keep its technical lead in many facets of integrated circuit technology by confining what joint research has been necessary to one company at a time. In this way it has ensured that no other company really understands the state of NTT technology. Failure at the same time to participate in MITI-sponsored projects, however, has not deprived NTT of major government subsidies. In recent years, NTT has continually issued, as might be expected, government guaranteed bonds and has had loans from the Japanese postal savings system.

The VLSI program is not an isolated example. Japanese government interfirm cooperative research programs in flexible manufacturing systems (FMS), fifth generation computers, and in biogenetic engineering have all suffered from similar strains.[20] With flexible manufacturing systems, Yamazaki Seikō, the firm with the most advanced technology in this area, strenuously criticized the government-sponsored cooperative programs as aiming to research a project whose outcome would be a system less advanced than what Yamazaki Seikō was already capable of producing. Only strong pressure on the heavily leveraged Yamazaki Seikō by its bank forced its participation in a project it felt would be, at best, of no help, and at worst, highly detrimental to its interests![21] For the fifth generation computers project, Fujitsu's position was analogous to Yamazaki Seikō in FMS. Again, Fujitsu claimed to have many elements of the technology which the government's cooperative project was seeking to research and develop.

In all likelihood, Yamazaki Seikō's and Fujitsu's claims are correct, and it is equally likely that the relevant Ministry of International Trade and Industry bureau chiefs were well aware of the accuracy of their claims. It may well be that seeking more leakage of proprietary information than would otherwise be the case, MITI was not unhappy if these flows were in some instances decidedly one way.

It is often argued that Japanese government policy is anticompetitive insofar as market structure issues are concerned, and that this is in clear contrast with the procompetitive policies continually pursued by, for instance, the Anti-Trust Division of the U.S. Justice Department. For the United States, for much of its industrial history a giant in the world economy, a procompetitive policy could often only mean the scaling down and breaking up of its dominant firms. For Japan, however, until recently a small element in the global economy, a domestic procompetitive policy characteristically meant insuring that no one Japanese firm exclusively locked up for itself a potentially world class industry and technology. That the motivation for such a policy often sprang from the most sordid cross currents in inter-zaibatsu rivalries in no way diminishes its socially beneficial impact. On the basis of its tradition, and given the reaction of many Japanese firms, it seems sensible to hypothesize that the Japanese government-sponsored interfirm cooperative research programs are more a program of diffusing technology so that more Japanese firms can compete with world class technologies than they are programs pursuing advances over technological bottlenecks.

JAPANESE MARKET AND NONMARKET TRANSFERS OF TECHNOLOGY

While it is possible to think of Japanese industrial policy as a functional substitute for certain elements of American-style capital and labor markets, Japan's position for much of the postwar period as a technological follower presents an international context for Japanese industrial policy which does not have an easy analogue in recent American experience. If Japanese labor market practices built walls preventing information flows among Japanese firms which government policy has broken down only with difficulty, Japanese firms have not necessarily faced many more difficulties than have American firms in benefiting from the market and nonmarket diffusion of proprietary and nonproprietary information available within and without the American economy. In this connection many of the so-called reciprocity issues which are raised for Japanese trade in goods recur in a potentially even more dramatic way for technology flows.

Is Japan a technology and information sponge? Specialized university graduate training and research programs are, by their very nature, largely committed to the production and diffusion of nonproprietary information. The Japanese primary reliance on within-firm training has meant such programs are underdeveloped in Japan. When, during the postwar period, Japanese firms have needed the information produced in such programs they have had the opportunity to send their employees to study in the United States. For the most part, during the postwar period, a reciprocal reverse flow of American students going to Japan would simply not have made sense. Similarly, the much greater professional orientation of American personnel, and the selective disclosure of proprietary information by individuals, and even firms, for labor mobility purposes, both in print and more informally, has meant that it has made sense for Japanese firms and the Japanese government to maintain technological and economic listening posts in the United States. As much as the lower level of technological accomplishment, and more important than the language barrier, the relative lack of such formal and informal disclosures in Japan has made unnecessary, for much of the postwar period, the creation of similar American listening posts there.[22]

It is not simply that technology flows have been disproportionately one way because information has been openly available and that Japanese firms and their government developed the receptors to take advantage of this information. Much technological information has also been directly available through the market.

While it is not easy to measure the nonmarket flows of technology, analysis of even the market information which is available is extremely instructive. Many of the issues raised in connection with nonmarket transfers should be reflected in the market data. As Japan has been a heavy net purchaser of foreign technology throughout the postwar period, it is appropriate to ask whether Japanese levels of market imports and exports of technology services are large and small, respectively, given the level of domestic technology in Japan. Have Japanese restrictions via patents, informal means, or otherwise, prevented reciprocal exports of technology? Have Japanese restrictions on trade in goods greatly affected Japanese trade in technology services?

The same cross-national general equilibrium framework which has been used to examine trade in goods and is described in the Appendix can be used to examine whether the Japanese economy has exhibited distinctive behavior in its trade in technological services. Indeed, because Equation (A8) for technology services will have the same form and independent variables as Equation (A8) for goods, it is possible to get Aitken efficient estimates of both even while estimating them separately.

Equation (A8) is estimated for technology flows for eleven countries, for twenty-five different industrial sectors for the years 1965, 1973, 1975, 1977, and 1979. The eleven countries include Australia, Canada, France, Germany, Italy, Japan, Korea, the Netherlands, Sweden, and the United Kingdom, and the United States. In actual estimation only two of the Japanese country terms were found to be statistically significant. Japanese technology trade behavior did not differ markedly from what might have been expected given its resource endowment.[23]

CONCLUSION

The accumulation and the allocation of capital and labor skills has been institutionalized very differently in Japan and the United States. The long absence of American-style market allocation of capital in Japan necessitated an important government role. Japanese government industrial policy worked to minimize the social losses resulting from the concentration of capital in Japan even as it harnessed the energies of inter-zaibatsu rivalry to socially constructive ends. The government functioned as a substitute for, rather than as a complement to, market processes.

In the same way that industrial policy in Japan operated to ensure that the concentration of capital in Japan did not lead to a misallocation of resources, so also has complementary Japanese government science and technology policy worked to ensure that the barriers to interfirm transfer of information created by Japanese permanent employment practices have not slowed the pace of technology diffusion within Japan. The widely discussed Japanese government-sponsored comparative R&D projects must be understood as a substitute for what has been achieved in other industrialized economies, particularly in the United States, as a byproduct of a well-functioning market for experienced scientific and engineering manpower. These projects and related government policies have been efforts to ensure that barriers to informal interfirm transfer of information created by permanent employment have not worked to slow the pace of diffusion within Japan.

APPENDIX: A GENERAL EQUILIBRIUM MODEL OF TRADE STRUCTURE

Introduction

Too much of the discussion on the modern development of the Japanese economy stresses the special unique characteristics of Japan as explanations of this development. In turn, the aggressive Japanese business expansion pattern, the unique style of decision making, unusual business groupings, the special ways of handling the labor force, the clinging to traditional consumption patterns, the strength of the family in the context of loyalty to national symbols, the unique capacity to absorb from other cultures, have all been touted separately and collectively as a means of understanding what has happened during the last 120 years, and during the last 30 years. The basic thrust of this literature is not surprising. On the one hand, many, though certainly not all, of these explanations have been developed by many of the same individuals who have helped to establish Japanese studies as a separate field of inquiry in the United States. On the other hand, many Japanese, in an effort to change the discussion of commercial disputes from low wages and unfair trade practices, have also openly promoted explanations which have emphasized the superiority of distinctively Japanese behavior and practices.

It is hardly surprising or inappropriate that either group should emphasize the gains that can be derived from cultural considerations. Understanding of the Japanese economy cannot be entirely divorced from an intimate knowledge of Japanese personality, society, and culture, but surely the situation, at least in the policy context, has already gone too far. In the U.S. Congressional U.S.-Japan Trade Task Force Report issued September, 1980, it was suggested that "Japan is generally an open nation" but that "private (cultural?) barriers to trade are very serious and may account for billions of dollars in lost U.S. export opportunity."[24] Indeed, when the areas of the economy are listed where such barriers are important they turn out to cover some 73.5 percent of total Japanese manufactured imports. Can this be true? Is Japanese behavior really so distinctive in its economic consequences?

Given this perspective, and given the desire to pose the analysis in the broadest possible context to ultimately facilitate longterm forecasting, the empirical work which is undertaken here uses an analytical framework which is self-consciously comparative. This approach presumes that Japanese phenomena can be explained by theories which are general over time and space. It is hoped that Japanese phenomena can be explained in the context of general explanations which are relevant for all countries. The actual analytical framework used in this work is an adaptation of the Hecksher-Ohlin-Samuelson Theory of Comparative Advantage. This theory, a long-term favorite of undergraduate instructors of international trade, emphasizes that the structure and level of international trade can be explained by the distribution of inputs into the production process throughout the world's many economies. The original formulation of this model stressed the national availability of capital, labor, skills, social organization, and natural resources.

In the perspective of the 30 years since H-O-S first gained wide currency, this theory now seems a nit bit shopworn. Since the famous Leonteif Paradox results in 1953, numerous attempts have been made to verify the theory empirically. A review of this literature is curiously unsatisfying. The algebra of H-O-S has been worked in very great detail by a generation of pure trade economists. Strangely enough, however, testing of H-O-S often makes almost no direct use of this formal framework. Often the functional forms imposed in these tests cannot be derived from H-O-S mathematics.

It is occasionally suggested that the strong assumptions necessary to the development of the formal structure of H-O-S leave little doubt about the outcome of such a test. Such an attitude seems in some respects unscientific. Theories are generally judged by their explanatory power, not by the simplicity of their assumptions. In any event, by the standards of economic research the assumptions of (1) a single, homogeneous of degree of one production function for each world industry, and (2) identical worldwide preference structures, if properly understood, do not appear extreme. Rather, the reluctance to test H-O-S formally arises out of the implications of this theory.

The same structure which generates the H-O-S theory of comparative advantage in a form where estimation can take place by linear methods also necessitates that prices of inputs throughout the world should be identical. At first blush this is so clearly counterintuitive as to disparage the entire analysis. Wage rates for unskilled labor are very much higher in Japan than in India. Only when it is understood that, within a category such as unskilled labor, quality may vary sufficiently to account for observed international differences can the theory be rescued. This manner of rescue still creates problems for the empirical implementation of H-O-S. In order to use this framework in the context of econometric investigations, some means of assessing international differences in input quality must be established. One suspects it is this problem which is really responsible for making the empirical testing of pure trade theory so different from the testing of pure consumption or production theory. Below an approach to overcoming this roadblock is suggested. Once overcome, it will be found that H-O-S theory is highly appropriate as an explanatory and long-range forecasting framework. Among its many virtues are its general equilibrium nature and its relatively undemanding data requirements.

Formal Framework[25]

Supply. Suppose the technology of an economy may be summarized by a variable profit function.[26] Further suppose that this profit function is approximated by:

$$\pi(P,L) = \sum_{i=1}^{N} \sum_{j=1}^{N} \sum_{s=1}^{K} d_{is}(\tfrac{1}{2}P_i^2 + \tfrac{1}{2}P_j^2)^{\frac{1}{2}} a_s L_s$$

$$+ \sum_{i=1}^{N} \sum_{s=1}^{K} c_{is} P_i a_s L_s$$

$$+ \sum_{i=1}^{N} \sum_{s=1}^{K} \sum_{r=1}^{K} f_{sf}(a_s L_s)^{\frac{1}{2}} (a_r L_{4r})^{\frac{1}{2}} P_i \qquad \text{(A1)}$$

where:

$$\begin{aligned}
d_{is} &= d_{si} \\
f_{sr} &= f_{rs} \\
d_{ii} &= 0 \text{ for } i = 1,2,\ldots,N \\
f_{ss} &= 0 \text{ for } s = 1,2,\ldots,K \\
\pi &\equiv \text{profit function} \\
P &\equiv \text{price} \\
L &\equiv \text{factor of production} \\
a &\equiv \text{quality of factor} \\
c_{is}, d_{is} &\equiv \text{parameters of the profit function}
\end{aligned}$$

Using Hotelling's lemma, A.1 may be differentiated with respect to each of the output prices to obtain a system of derived supply functions.[27]

$$X_i(P,L) = \sum_{j=1}^{N} \sum_{s=1}^{K} d_{ij} (\tfrac{1}{2}P_i^2 + \tfrac{1}{2}P_j^2)^{-\frac{1}{2}} P_i a_s L_s$$

$$+ \sum_{s=1}^{K} c_{is} a_s L_s + \sum_{s=1}^{K} \sum_{r=1}^{K} f_{sr} (a_s L_s)^{\frac{1}{2}} (a_r L_r)^{\frac{1}{2}} \qquad \mathrm{i} = 1,2,\ldots,N$$

$$= \sum_{s=1}^{K} Q_{is} a_s L_s + \sum_{s=1}^{K} \sum_{r=1}^{K} f_{sr} (a_s L_s)^{\frac{1}{2}} (a_r L_r)^{\frac{1}{2}}$$

$$= \sum_{s=1}^{K} Q_{is} a_s L_s + \sum_{s=1}^{K} \sum_{r=1}^{K} f_{sr} (a_s a_r)^{\frac{1}{2}} L_s^{\frac{1}{2}} L_r^{\frac{1}{2}} \qquad i = 1,2,\ldots,N \qquad \text{(A2)}$$

where $Q_{is} \equiv \sum_{j=1}^{N} d_{ij} (\tfrac{1}{2}P_i^1 + \tfrac{1}{2}P_j^2)^{-\frac{1}{2}} P_i + c_{is}$

and $X_i \equiv i^{\text{th}}$ good or service

Provided the much debated Law of One Price holds and the price of a particular good is everywhere the same, the Q_{is} may be treated as constant and Equation A2 can be used as a framework to explain cross-national sectoral economic activity. Sectoral economic performance is in this way tied to aggregate factor availability. If it is also assumed that the Factor Price Equalization Theorem holds up to a multiplicative quality differential, then by using Hotelling's lemma the second partial derivatives of the profit function with respect to factor endowments must be zero if factor price equalization is to occur.[28] Applying Hotelling's lemma:

$$a_s w_s = \delta\pi(P,L)/\delta(a^s L_s) \qquad s = 1,\ldots,K \qquad \text{(A3)}$$

where $w_s \equiv s^{\text{th}}$ factor reward

$$\frac{\delta(a_s w_s)}{\delta(a_s L_s)} = \frac{\delta\pi(P,L)}{\delta(a_s L_s)^2} = 0 \qquad s = 1,\ldots,K \qquad \text{(A4)}$$

or from Equation (A1):

$$\tfrac{1}{2} f_{rs}(a_s L_s)^{-\frac{1}{2}} (a_r L_r)^{-\frac{1}{2}} \left(\sum_{i=1}^{I} P_i\right) = 0 \qquad \text{(A5)}$$

This, in turn, implies $f_{rs} = 0$ and

$$X_i(L) = \sum_{s=1}^{K} Q_{js} a_s L_s \qquad \text{(A6)}$$

Demand. The framework for obtaining trade structure as opposed to just output structure requires a demand side. Assume an indirect trade utility exists that expresses the maximum level of utility an open economy can obtain as a function of a vector of prices for commodities, a vector of factor endowments, and the balance of trade.[29] The indirect trade utility can be defined concretely in terms of the ordinary trade utility function and the variable profit (or GNP) function in Equation (A2). When this is done, following the approach taken in the previous section, an extension of Roy's Identity can be developed that allows the easy generation of net export functions by differentiation. It it is assumed, as in the previous section, that commodity prices are equalized by trade and that technology is homogeneous and identical across economies up to multiplicative quality differentials in inputs and if, in addition, it is assumed that national preferences are homothetic, but not necessarily identical, then the net export function can be written analogously to Equation (A2) in a form that is linear in the parameters and that can be estimated econometrically. If the generalized Leontief form is imposed not only on the supply side, as in Equation (A1), but also on the demand side, the following general form of net export function emerges:

$$E_i = \sum_{s=1}^{K} B_{is}(a_s L_s) + \sum_{s=1}^{K} \sum_{r=1}^{K} H_{irs}({}_sL_s)^{½}(a_r L_r)^{½} \qquad i = 1,\ldots,N \qquad \text{(A7)}$$

where $E_i \equiv$ net exports of ith good or service.

$$B_{is} \equiv G_{is} - Q_{is} \text{ where } G_{is} \equiv \frac{w_s \sum_{j=1} b_{ij} P_i^{-½} P_j^{½}}{\sum_{h=1}^{N} \sum_{m=1}^{N} b_{km} P_k^{½} P_m^{½}}$$

$$H_{irs} \equiv f_{rs}$$

As in the previous section, if it is also assumed that the Factor Price Equalization Theorem holds up to a multiplicative quality term, then international trade will equalize factor prices per unit of factor quality and, as before, the H_{irs} in Equation A7 will equal zero. This simplifies Equation A7 to the extent that:[30]

$$E_i = \sum_{i=s}^{K} B_{is}(a_s L_s) \qquad i = 1,\ldots,N \qquad \text{(A8)}$$

Equation A7 or A8 can be used as a framework to explain structural change in an economy's international trade.

Estimation. Equation (A8) is to be estimated for N commodity groups from international cross section data. Were it not for unknown variations in the quality of inputs across countries, estimation of Equation (A8) might proceed using ordinary least squares methods. Formally, the estimation of Equation A8 with a_s differing across countries and unknown *is* a multivariate errors in a variable problem.[31] Instrumental variable methods will allow consistent estimation of the B_{is}. For any given commodity cross section a_s will not be identified. In the particular specification adopted here, however, at any given time, there are i cross sections that contain the identical independent variables. This happy circumstance will permit consistent estimation of the a_x for each economy.[32] These estimates of a_s can then be used to obtain new Aitken efficient estimates of B_{is}.

NOTES AND REFERENCES

1. Ryutarō Komiya "Economic Planning in Japan," in *Economic Planning: East and West,* ed. Morris Bornstein. Cambridge, MA: Ballinger, 1973.

2. Lester Thurow, *The Zero Sum Society* (New York: Basic Books, 1980).

3. Good general reviews of this literature are included in Charles E. Lindblom, *Politics, Economics, and Markets* (New York: Basic Books, 1977); and William Baumol, *The Stock Market and Economic Efficiency* (New York: Fordham University Press, 1967). For more recent discussions, see Eugene F. Fama, *Foundations of Finance* (New York: Basic Books, 1976); G. William Schwert, "Using Financial Data to Measure Effects of Regulation," *Journal of Law and Economics* (April 1981), and Marjorie A. Flavin, "Excess Volatility in the Financial Markets: A Reassessment of the Empirical Evidence," *Journal of Political Economy* (December 1983).

4. R. Pascale and J. Athos, *The Art of Japanese Management* (New York: Simon & Shuster, 1991); R. Hayes and T. Abernathy, "Managing Our Way to Economic Decline," *Harvard Business Review* (July-August 1980).

5. The 10-K filings with the Securities and Exchange Commission by publicly traded companies in the United States must contain some detail on the compensation agreements with top corporate officers.

6. This is pointed out explicitly in D. Jorgenson and Z. Griliches, "The Explanation of Productivity Changes," *Review of Economic Studies* (July 1967).

7. H. Chenery, "Patterns of Industrial Growth" *American Economic Review* (March 1961).

8. The modern production theory made use of is described in W.E. Diewert, "Application of Duality Theory," in *Frontiers of Quantitative Economics,* Vol. II, M.D. Intriligator and D.A. Kendrick (eds.) (New York, 1974). Related versions of these results can be found in Gary R. Saxonhouse, "What's Wrong with Japanese Trade Structure?" *Pacific Economic Papers* 136 (June 1986): 1-36; and Gary R. Saxonhouse, "Differentiated Products, Economies of Scale and Access to the Japanese Market," in *Trade Policies for International Competitiveness,* Robert Feenstra (ed.) (Chicago, 1989). See also Edward F. Leamer, *Sources of Comparative Advantage* (Cambridge, MA., 1984).

9. To the extent that public subsidies were important in keeping down tuition in higher education in Japan and the United States, students were not totally reliant on their own resources. In prewar Japan, as in postwar Japan, such benefits were limited to a relatively small group of individuals. In the prewar United States, public education with public subsidy was much more broadly available, but if the cost of training includes wages foregone plus living expenses, plus tuition, even this subsidy was relatively small.

10. The Japanese government's early efforts to subsidize private universities are reviewed in Akiyoshi Horiuchi, "Daigaku kyōiku no rieki, hiyō oyobi hojokin—Nihon ni tsuite no jishoteki kentō," *Nippon rōdō kyōkai zasshi* (April 1973).

11. See the discussion in Gary R. Saxonhouse, "Country Girls and Communication among Competitors in the Japanese Cotton Spinning Industry," in Hugh Patrick (ed.), *Japanese Industrialization and Its Social Consequences* (Berkeley, CA: 1976).

12. A permanent employment program, particularly with heavily seniority-related wage and salary scales is made far more feasible than it otherwise might be through the simultaneous existence of a somewhat profit-sensitive bonus for both white and blue collar workers, which is in normal periods some 30 to 40 percent of total compensation. In Japan, it is possible to meet disequilibrium through price as well as quantity adjustment in factor markets.

13. Since in Japan training institutions underwrite training costs and hope to directly recoup them, there is much less likelihood of investment and social waste in the accumulation of economically unneeded skills.

14. In light of this analysis, it is surprising that D. Eleanor Westney and Kiyonori Sakakibara, "Comparative Study of the Training, Careers and Organization of Engineers in the Computer Industry in the United States and Japan," *M.I.T.-Japan Science and Technology Program Working Paper,* in a survey they conduct, find that Japanese engineers claim to care more about their extra-firm reputation than do their American counterparts.

15. D. Eleanor Westney and Kihonori Sakakibara, "Comparative Study of Training, Careers and Organization of Engineers in the Computer Industry in the United States and Japan," find that Japanese and American engineers do allocate their time in statistically significantly different ways.

16. Japanese research associations are most typically special entities for tax purposes. Firms which are members of government-authorized research associations can take a 100 percent depreciation deduction for all fixed assets used in connection with association activities. Many Japanese research associations, such as the Electric Car Research Association, are formed for very specific joint R&D ventures and actually have no joint laboratories.

17. There are presently about 30 research associations operating in Japan.

18. Daniel I. Okimoto, "Pioneer and Pursuer: The Role of the State in the Evolution of the Japanese and American Semiconductor Industries," *Northeast Asia-United States Forum on International Policy Occasional Paper* (April 1983).

19. The Post Office was also able to protect NTT from MITI pressures during the epic Government Procurement Code Controversy during the closing weeks of the GATT Tokyo Round negotiations.

20. See also the discussion in Gary R. Saxonhouse, "Biotechnology in Japan: Industrial Policy and Factor Market Distortions," *Prometheus* (December 1985): 277-314.

21. Gary R. Saxonhouse, "The National Security Clause of the Trade Expansion Act of 1962: Import Competition and the Machine Tool Industry," In Gary R. Saxonhouse and Kozo Yamamura (eds.), *Law and Trade Issues of the Japanese Economy* (Seattle, WA, 1986).

22. In recent years, the number of research papers published by Japanese scientists and engineers, and the number of international citations of their work, has greatly increased. As noted in Daniel Okimoto and Gary R. Saxonhouse, "Technology and the Future of the Japanese Economy," in Tahashi Inoguchi and Daniel Okimoto (eds.), *The Political Economy of Japan* (Stanford, CA: 1987) Japan still ranks well behind the U.S. performance.

23. The sample used in this estimation and the results obtained are reported in more detail in Gary R. Saxonhouse, "Services in the Japanese Economy," in Robert Inman (ed.), *Managing the Services Economy: Prospects and Problems* (Cambridge: Cambridge University Press, 1985), pp. 53-83.

24. Subcommittee on Trade, Committee on Ways and Means, U.S. House of Representatives, *U.S.-Japan Trade Report* (Washington, 1980). For recent versions of this approach see James Fallows, "Containing Japan,' *The Atlantic* (May 1989); Chalmers Johnson, "Their Behavior, Our Policy," *The National Interest* (Fall 1989).

25. A framework similar to what is proposed here has been used in exploring international trade in goods. See Gary Saxonhouse, "The Micro- and Macroeconomics of Foreign Sales to Japan," in William Cline (ed.), *Trade Policy for the 1980s* (Cambridge, MA, 1983); Gary Saxonhouse, "Evolving Comparative Advantage and Japan's Imports of Manufactures," in Kozo Yamamura (ed.), *Policy and Trade Issues of the Japanese Economy* (Seattle, WA, 1982); and, more recently, Gary R. Saxonhouse, "Product Differentiation, Economies of Scale and Access to the Japanese Market," in Robert Feenstra (ed.), *Trade Policies for International Competitiveness* (Chicago, 1989).

26. The concept of a variable profit function was first suggested by Paul A. Samuelson, "Price of Factors and Goods in General Equilibrium, *Review of Economic Studies* 21 (June 1953).

27. Hotelling's lemma is discussed in W.M. Gorman, "Measuring the Quantities of Fixed Factors," in J.N. Wolfe (ed.), *Value Capital and Growth* (Chicago, 1968).

28. In what follows empirical work will proceed as if $N = K$, despite the number of inputs for which data are available being almost 100 less than the number of goods. Given the rather arbitrary aggregation and disaggregation in goods and factors in empirical work of this kind, it is appropriate to assume that the number of goods and input are many and that included and excluded dependent and independent variables have properties such that exclusion of relevant variables does not bias estimation of the coefficients for included variables.

29. This formulation rests critically on the existence of direct community utility functions. For the conditions under which this might be true see Paul A.

Samuelson, "Social Indifference Curves," *Quarterly Journal of Economics* February 1956); and E. Eisenberg, "Aggregation of Utility Functions," *Management Science* (July 1961). Early applications upon which the current analyses are built include Gary R. Saxonhouse, "Evolving Comparative Advantage and Japan's Imports of Manufactures," in Kozo Yamamura (ed.), *Policy and Trade Issues of the Japanese Economy* (Seattle, WA, 1982); and Gary R. Saxonhouse, "The Micro- and Macroeconomics of Foreign Sales to Japan," in William Cline (ed.), *Trade Policy for the 1980s* (Cambridge, MA, 1983).

30. The estimation of a version of Equation A7 is discussed in Gary R. Saxonhouse, "Evolving Comparative Advantage and Japan's Imports of Manufactures." The estimation of Equation (A8) is discussed in Gary R. Saxonhouse, "The Micro- and Macroeconomics of Foreign Sales to Japan."

31. In actual estimation an additive error term for equations will also be assumed.

32. For example, let $a_s = 1 + a'_s$. Using instrumental variable techniques in the presence of multiplicative errors allows consistent estimation of the B_{is}. Using these estimates, for each economy and $N \times L$ vector $[v_i]'$ of commodity equation residuals can be formed for each time period. Consistent estimates of the quality terms for each country for each time period can then be obtained from:

$$\{[B_{is}L_s]' \, [B_{is}L_s]\}^{-1} \, \{[B_{is}L_s]' \, [v_i]\}.$$

INDUSTRIAL POLICY AND THE DIFFUSION OF KNOWLEDGE

Gerald Nickelsburg

The analysis of Saxonhouse of the Japanese experience with industrial policy illustrates two popular views of the Japanese development in the postwar era. First, that industrial policy is a substitute for, and not a complement to, free market development and second, that Japan was destined to develop rapidly in the absence of industrial policy. This analysis is not convincing, because it precludes by definition the possibility of industrial policy being a positive force in overcoming externalities and fostering efficient growth. In this paper we present a model in which the "no effect" result is nested and therefore testable. We believe that such analysis will help in more careful interpretation of industrial policy issues.

The issue of industrial policy has in recent years become the focus of much policy discussion. On one hand, there are many who point to the Japanese experience with an industrial planning board, MITI, as an example of successful industrial policy (Thurow, 1980 and Vogel, 1980 are examples of this school of thought). On the other, many economists point out that there exist other explanations for Japan's rapid growth in the postwar years and that Japanese industrial policy could at best be benign, but probably it retarded the rate of economic growth (for example Krugman, 1983; Saxonhouse, 1985; Summers, 1983). This point of view, which is neoclassicist, rests primarily on the welfare propositions of competitive analysis. However, there is a sense in which market interventions are appropriate in this framework. In this paper we present a model which formalizes the market structure externality approach to industrial policy and then reinterprets Japanese industrial policy as an attempt to compete "fairly"—that is, on the same basis as the rest of the world. We wish to point out at the start, however, that this is an exercise in economic theory, and its veracity for the Japanese experience requires an empirical implementation of our model.

The main thrust of the industrial policy debate in the United States has revolved around proposals for a national planning board of some kind. Such proposals, in fact, are proposals for a new mercantilism, and ignore the gains which accrue to market allocations of resources. By attempting to target new, "successful" industries, the industrial policy camp is in effect attempting to replace market outcomes with planned outcomes. If we follow the line of reasoning of Thurow and others we must therefore, conclude that industrial policy is nothing more than a redistributive device which will lower national income in general, and which does not hold out the promise of accomplishing its redistributive goal.

However, if one takes seriously the notion that market structures are different in different countries, and that at present we may be obtaining second best allocations with the present international trade framework, then an analysis of the potential gains and losses to industrial policy need to be framed in rigorous models so that the appropriate second best solutions to the allocation of resources may be found. It is only in this way that industrial policy makes sense in terms of creating conditions for rapid economic growth.

We present one example of this kind of reasoning. Basically, we propose a model of Japanese and U.S. research and development (R&D) in the context of world trade. Because of the different structures of the market, and because the output of R&D is observable while many aspects of inputs to the production process are not, the net result is a free market allocation which is suboptimal. As a result, market interventionist policies, perhaps cooperative between governments, are required to restore optimality.

THE MODEL

To formalize the idea of innovation, without requiring each to be distinct, we define an innovation as the production of a good which yields a stream of income. However, the innovation technology diffuses at a rate per unit time and therefore does not provide a permanent stream of income. We assume that only firms produce innovations and that the production requires labor, capital resources, and effort, and that the production function contains a random shock. Formally, we write:

$$I = F(K,L,E,U) \quad (1)$$

where I is the output innovation, K is capital, L is labor, E is effort, and U an id random component. The firm is assumed to receive a flow of income from the innovation I equal to in present value:

$$PV = I \, \frac{1 + r}{(1 + r - v)} \quad (2)$$

where v is the rate of technology diffusion and r is the rate of time preference. Firms pay the rental rate r, which is equal to the rate of time preference for capital and the real wage w to labor. However, firms cannot observe E as distinct from U, and therefore cannot compensate workers directly for the input of effort. In order to induce workers to provide effort, firms pay the bonus B to workers based on the output I.

There are two other goods, X and Y, which are traded internationally without barriers to trade. Following Heckscher-Ohlin we assume neoclassical production functions and competitive markets. Therefore, there is one unique world price ratio and the relative price of factors is given as:

$$w/r = G^i_{LX}/G^i_{KX} = G^i_{LY}/G^i_{KY} \tag{3}$$

where G is the production function for X and Y, i denotes country, and the subscript denotes partial derivative or marginal product.

The good I is nontraded in our model, except that it is assumed to enhance the production of good X and good Y by providing lower costs and temporary rents. That is, production of I provides to the firm a proportionate increase in average products, and therefore pure profit to the firm. In a more general setting we would want to consider the effect of such technology on market share, as well as on the dynamic international allocation of income between the two countries.

AN ANALYSIS OF EQUILIBRIA

We begin our analysis by specifying the firm's problem. For the production of the two goods X and Y the problem is straightforward and well-known. Therefore we need not repeat it here. For the production of the rent-generating innovation, we assume the firm is a risk neutral expected profit maximizer. Therefore, the firm chooses levels of L and K as inputs and B as a bonus for effort to maximize subject to Equations (1) and (2):

$$E\,PV - wL - rk - B\,E\,I \tag{4}$$

where E is taken to mean the mathematical expectation with respect to U. Substituting into (4) we find the first order conditions:

$$E\,F_K = r\,\left(\frac{1+r}{1+r-v} - B\right)^{-1} \tag{5}$$

$$E\,F_L = w\,\left(\frac{1+r}{1+r-v} - B\right)^{-1}$$

$$\left(\frac{1+r}{1+r-v} - B\right)\phi(B)\,E\,F_E = 0$$

where ϕ is the partial derivative of E with respect to B.

From Equation (5) we have two immediate results. First, the ratio of expected marginal products of capital and labor is the rental/wage ratio, and since this is identical across countries, the proportion of capital to labor employed in the production of R&D is optimal in an expected value sense. Second, the amount paid to workers for effort, B, is a function of the diffusion rate v. From the third first order condition of Equation (5) we have:

$$B = \theta(K, L, 1 + r, v). \tag{6}$$

Now, the rate of diffusion need not be the same across countries. This rate is structurally and culturally determined, since the diffusion of technology is, in its most basic form, the emission of information. If workers feel a loyalty towards their firm, or if there exist no incentives to publicize their findings in research, and perhaps even social pressure not to, then the rate of diffusion ($1 - v$) will be quite low. On the other hand, if social or cultural norms are not so strict, or if it is profitable to publicize an innovation, the rate of diffusion could be quite high.

With differing rates (v), firms in the two countries would pay workers different bonuses (B) for the provision of effort. Let us suppose, for example, that country J has a low diffusion rate and country A has a high diffusion rate. Then $B_j > B_A$ and the absolute level of E for given K and L will be different for the two countries. Indeed, even though:

$$E\, F_K^J \,/\, E\, F_L^J = E\, F_K^A \,/\, E\, F_L^A$$

because of the identical wage rental ratios, the input ratios of K to L are going to be different in the two countries.

In other words, the existence of two distinct rates of diffusion of technology creates two distinct production functions for the same good, I. Obviously this is a source of inefficiency in the world economy, since with the same input prices, the efficient producer of I should be specialized in producing I with gains reallocated across borders.

Under conditions of a subsidy to R&D the equilibrium obviously changes. Suppose that country J employs a subsidy τ to the R&D

process. Then, if this is tied to worker bonuses and passed completely onto the worker, the optimal level of B is given by:

$$\theta(B + \tau) = (\frac{1 + r}{1 + r - v} + \tau - B) \quad (7)$$

With this subsidy we still have $E\ F_K/\ E\ F_L - r/w$, but the input mix of k to L has changed. Indeed, for each subsidy τ there is a different input mix. It then follows that under standard optimality conditions there exists a τ such that the two production functions are identical and that all of the conditions for world optimality are satisfied. In this way industrial policy can play an important role in eliminating structural differences.

A POSSIBLE REINTERPRETATION

One of the arguments advanced for extensive use of industrial planning in Japan (see Vogel and Chambers), and which is being advanced in many LDCs today, in that industrial policy is necessary if domestic producers are to be able to "fairly" compete in world markets. The rationale behind this argument is that many aspects of domestic markets are not well developed, for example domestic equity and capital markets, domestic insurance markets, or domestic technology production markets. As a consequence, completely free trade will leave them consigned to an inferior position with respect to many newly emerging industries and an inability to change their comparative advantage in a changing world environment. This is tantamount to consigning themselves to be producers of primary products, goods for which many good substitutes exist.

The beginnings of a theory presented above illustrate how this argument could be made rigorous. In Japan after the World War II, capital markets were quite thin and the ability to generate new products, to be a competitor on new product frontiers, seemed nonexistent. This may well be found empirically to characterize a situation where there was a rate of product diffusion which was much different from its primary trading partner, the United States. If so, then the use of industrial policy to modernize its industry, and in particular to obtain a growth pattern which provided comparative advantage in new products, may only have been a policy to eliminate certain barriers to truly competitive behavior. This can be true even though Japanese barriers seem to have been anticompetitive and anti-free trade because they could have been creating the environment which would have existed had there been initially identical structures across the country.

In this sense, industrial policy would clearly have been beneficial, which it seems to have been. The results of Saxonhouse and those of Krugman, which suggest competitive market allocations have occurred in spite of industrial policy, are consistent, and possibly more plausibly reinterpreted in light of our results. In particular, we may find empirically that market outcomes that are predicted by competitive market theory are what has occurred. But, in the absence of industrial policy these outcomes may not have occurred. Consequently, advocacy of industrial policy requires solving this identification problem and delineating for each situation the existence of clear gains in national welfare. Finally, these results suggest that it would be difficult for the United States to duplicate MITI experience unless we can identify similar sources of market inefficiency.

REFERENCES

Johnson, C. 1982. *MITI and The Japanese Miracle: The Growth of Industrial Policy*. Stanford, CA: Stanford University Press.

Krugman, P. 1983. "Targeted Industrial Policies: Theory and Evidence." Pp. 123-155 in *Industrial Change and Public Policy*. Federal Reserve Bank of Kansas City.

Saxonhouse, G.R. 1985. "Japanese High Technology, Government Policy, and Evolving Comparative Advantage in Goods and Services." In *Industrial Policy and International Trade,* edited by V. Canto and K. Dietrich. Greenwich, CT: JAI Press.

Thurow, L. 1980. *The Zero Sum Society*. New York: Basic Books.

Vogel, E.F. 1979. *Japan as Number One, Lessons for the United States.* Cambridge, MA: Harvard University Press.

TRADING POLICY OUTLOOK

Arthur B. Laffer

In every Presidency, several decisions prove to have an impact and importance which outlive the issues, the administration, and even the era. Our history is written by the most epic of these decisions. The Louisiana Purchase by Jefferson, the Emancipation Proclamation by Lincoln, the signing of the Smoot-Hawley Tariffs by Hoover, and the Marshall Plan by Truman are but four such decisions which shaped the destiny of the United States.

For most Presidents, such decisions are on a far less grand scale—severing the dollar/gold link by Nixon, maintaining price controls on petroleum products by Ford, and deferring the tax cut by Reagan, are but three important examples. These decisions formed a watershed, reverberating through the economy for many years: A monetary policy as successful as Bretton Woods has yet to be created; the benefits of oil price decontrol were postponed seven years; and deferral of the tax cut contributed directly to the severity of the 1982 recession.

President Reagan's action on steel import quotas had all the makings of another decision that would impact policy for years go come. The immediate stakes seemed narrow: The U.S. International Trade Commission (ITC) had recommended that import quotas and additional tariffs be imposed on foreign steel in five major steel product areas for the next five years.[1] This protection from foreign competition would be contingent upon the domestic steel industry's demonstrating a willingness to reduce costs, including wages, and to modernize its facilities. But the scope of the proposal indicated that the tone, if not the substance, of trade policy for the remainder of the decade might well be established by how Reagan's ruling on the ITC recommendation.

- For the first time, quotas would be imposed upon all foreign steel. Previously, limits on foreign steel had been imposed on a country by country basis.
- Steel's role as a major raw material input, and as a significant factor in world trade, suggest the ramifications of the steel decision extend well beyond the domestic steel industry.
- For the first time, trade restrictions were being linked directly to periodic government review and approval of the industry's "rehabilitation" program. Such supervision is far from benign, and can easily turn malignant. It increases the government's role in making important economic decisions and raises the stakes government officials have in the program's success or failure. The problem is that government rarely faces up to failure, and even less frequently achieves success when attempting to bail out an inefficient industry.
- The steel industry is but the cutting edge of growing protectionism in the United States. Protecting U.S. steel makers from foreign competition is central to the Democratic Party's restrictionist trade plank. Autos, copper, textiles, machine tools, and others are already lining up to receive protection similar to that now recommended for the steel industry.
- Passage of slightly different versions of the Simpson-Mazzoli immigration bill by the House and Senate demonstrated the popularity of protectionism in Washington. The legislation sought to curtail foreign individuals from working in the United States.

THE TRADE BALANCE AND THE ECONOMY

Ironically, the growing push for protectionism is due, in part, to the success of the Reagan Administration's economic program. Pressures for trade restrictions typically rise when the trade balance deteriorates. And a country's trade balance tends to deteriorate when its economy grows faster than the rest of the world. When a country is growing at an above average rate, it tends to acquire more goods and services (consumption) and capital goods (investment) than it produces. The difference is net imports from the rest of the world as foreign suppliers provide the excess goods, services, and capital goods in exchange for future claims (bonds and stocks) against the output of the U.S. economy.

It is precisely this phenomenon that has been ignited by the Reagan tax cuts. U.S. and non-U.S. investors alike have responded to the U.S. tax cuts by seeking to increase their investments in the United States. During 1983, U.S. citizens' ownership of assets abroad increased by only $49 billion, $69 billion less than in 1982 and the lowest capital outflow since 1977. By implication, U.S. citizens in 1983 made a greater proportion of their investment in the United States and a smaller proportion outside of the United States than in previous years. At the same time, foreign investment in the United States remained under its highs. In 1983, foreign ownership of assets in the United States increased by $83 billion, $4.8 billion less than the 1982 record, but $44.3 billion above its 1980 low point.

The difference between the increase of foreign-owned assets in the United States ($83 billion), and the increase in U.S.-owned assets abroad ($49 billion) is equal to the net inflow of foreign capital into the United States.

For all practical purposes, the U.S. and foreign central banks do not intervene in foreign exchange markets. As a result, the capital inflow induced by foreign investors must be matched dollar for dollar by a trade balance deficit[2]—the much disparaged deterioration in the trade account is accommodating the non-U.S. investors' desire to increase their ownership of U.S. assets. Capital and goods to where the action is.

Thus, the recent deterioration of the U.S. trade account is a result of the strength of the U.S. economy. It is a symptom of success:

- U.S. industrial production advanced 13.5 percent for the 12 months ending in May. Japan and Canada were the only other countries to post double digit advances—11.8 percent and 10.1 percent respectively.
- Employment gains in the United States also outrank by wide margins gains posted in the other industrial countries.
- In 1983, manufacturing productivity in the United States was up 6.2 percent—better than Germany or Japan, better than the U.S. average for the decade of the 1960s and clearly better than the average of the last ten years.
- The economic expansion has coincided with a larger than expected increase in investments. During the first five quarters of the expansion, real nonresidential investment has increased 17 percent. By contrast, personal consumption expenditures over these same five quarters have grown 7 percent.
- During the first five quarters of the recovery, merchandise exports grew at a seasonally adjusted annual rate of 9.4 percent. The large drop in merchandise exports occurred during the 1982 recession. Between the fourth quarter of 1981 and the fourth quarter of 1982, merchandise exports declined $9.3 billion to a low of $48.2 billion. By the first quarter of 1984, these exports had climbed to $54.1 billion. The expansion of the merchandise trade deficit during this period was due to an even larger ($20.2 billion) increase in imports.

THE PLIGHT OF THE STEEL INDUSTRY

That the once proud steel industry was leading the charge for trade restrictions during such a surge in investment and economic activity is itself powerful testimony to the failure of trade restrictions to help even an individual industry.

Few industries have been provided as much protection from foreign competition as has the steel industry.[3] Fifteen years ago, the villain was Japan. Voluntary Restraint Agreements (VRAs) with the Japanese and Europeans were negotiated to stem the steadily growing market share of foreign steel. The VRAs expired in 1974. In 1978, trigger prices, a form of minimum price for imported steel based on the efficient Japanese steel industry's production costs, were imposed. However, even this guard against low priced foreign steel failed as foreign steel companies, many of which are subsidized, cut prices in the face of shrinking demand. During 1981, foreign steel increased its market share to 19.1 percent from 16.3 percent in 1980. On average, steel production in 1981 was slightly higher than in 1980. But that disguised the trend: The U.S. operating rate declined to 58.6 percent in December 1981 from 77.8 percent in the previous December.

In response to this combination of falling output and eroding market share, the steel industry sought higher tariffs and other restrictions on steel imports from European and other foreign steel makers. This effort aggravated a rapidly deteriorating situation as foreign steel makers increased their deliveries in advance of any restrictions or penalties. Between January and September of 1982, foreign steel shipments captured 24 percent of the U.S. market and domestic operating rates declined to 39.8 percent, their lowest level since 1936.

In October 1982, the United States finalized negotiations to impose quotas on European steel imports in lieu of imposing countervailing and penalty duties. As a result, European steel imports were limited to about 85 percent of their 1981 levels.

But once again trade restrictions failed to deliver their promise of a healthier domestic steel industry. Such targeted restrictions are like the rock in the middle of a river. The world supply of steel simply moves around the restrictions much as water moves around an obstacle that only partially blocks its flow. Trade patterns may shift, but the location of steel production is left essentially unchanged.[4] There is a swirl of distortions at the point of interference, but little is changed downstream.

In the case of the steel quotas, European steel shipments to the United States were curtailed by the quotas. During 1983, imports of European steel mill products fell 1.5 million tons. But, imports of steel from Latin America—an area not covered by the quota—

increased 1.4 million tons to 2.4 million tons, while imports from Korea increased 700,000 tons. Overall, imports of steel mill products rose 407,000 tons.

The steel industry's response was to ask for the equivalent of a dam to be placed across the river of imports, regulating the flow of steel into the United States, regardless of its source. The ITC's recommendation would attempt to achieve precisely that result. Such a comprehensive policy, if skillfully designed and competently administered, could change the flow of steel mill products into the United States. Even in this case, however, it is far from clear that the steel industry would be made better off. The more successful the restrictions in isolating the U.S. market from the world steel market, the greater the incentives to cut new channels of distribution for foreign steel.

Bethlehem Steel Corporation estimated the quotas would produce a 10 percent price increase for steel sold in the United States, and generate approximately $2 billion in cash flow to the domestic industry. The net effect was to quantify, if only imprecisely, the payoff to circumventing the steel quotas. Three possibilities suggested themselves:

1. Increase imports of semifinished steel. Last year, slightly more than 750,000 tons of semifinished steel was imported by U.S. steel makers for finishing into various steel sheet and plate products. This channel, however, would be limited. The ITC recommended a 15 percent tariff be imposed on imports of semifinished steel in excess of 1.5 million tons. This tariff would be reduced to 10 percent in years four and five of the restrictions.
2. Increased imports of fabricated steel. Users of domestic steel will suddenly find they are suffering from a cost disadvantage vis-à-vis their non-U.S. competition that can purchase steel at the lower world price. As a result, imports of products intensive in the use of steel, from machine tools to automobiles and major home appliances, would be expected to increase. In addition, to the extent possible, users of steel products will find it to their advantage to source more steel parts from outside the United States. The auto

companies, for example, would be expected to increase purchases of components made of steel from their Canadian, European and, eventually, Asian operations.

3. Decreased exports of fabricated steel. U.S. producers intensive in the use of steel would also find themselves at a competitive disadvantage in their respective export markets. Again, sales of goods produced in U.S. facilities would decline. And, to the extent possible, U.S. companies would be expected to shift production outside of the United States.

It was as likely as not that trade restrictions once again would fail to improve the profitability of the steel industry or increase the employment of steel workers. The week the ITC recommended quotas, for example, the Standard and Poor's (S&P) Steel Index posted a slight decline relative to the S&P 500, indicating that the trade restrictions would not materially benefit the industry.

And it was a virtual certainty that imposition of worldwide steel quotas would reduce overall U.S. employment and corporate profits. On the day of the ITC announcement, the Dow Jones industrials fell 18.33 points. It was the sharpest one day decline since the raft of restrictionist news reached the market earlier this year.[5]

On the face of it, the political considerations seemed to dictate doing "something" to protect the steel industry. Thirty six states produce steel, and the nine largest producers—Indiana, Ohio, Pennsylvania, Michigan, Illinois, Kentucky, New York, California, and Texas—have a total of 225 electoral votes.[6] Democratic presidential nominee Walter Mondale had already actively campaigned for protecting the domestic steel industry.

Upon closer inspection, it was far from clear that moving to co-opt Mondale on the trade issue would enhance Reagan's or the Republicans' chances of victory in November. In the primary campaign, for example, Gary Hart explicitly rejected the call for protectionism, saying it would cost more jobs than it would save. Hart, against great odds, nearly matched Mondale in the popular vote.

The issue before President Reagan went well beyond steel to embrace the path of his administration's trade policy. At issue was whether the Administration would flirt with the politics of protectionism or devise a strategy to counter the protectionist urge.

The risk of flirtation is entrapment. Protectionism is seductive in its promise of saving American jobs. But the promise is a false one. Inefficient industries can be protected only to the disadvantage of the industries and consumers they serve. The inevitable consequence is fewer jobs and a lower standard of living for all.

The opportunity in devising an alternative to protectionism is to strengthen further the economic expansion and the Republicans' performance at the polls. In 1932, Franklin Delano Roosevelt defeated Herbert Hoover, in part, by calling for a reduction in the Republican-imposed trade restrictions. Good economics can be good politics.

The President, his administration, and the Republican Party were perfectly positioned to reject the ITC's recommendation. President Reagan had always been a strong advocate of free trade. In addition, the steel industry itself was in an upswing, thanks to the general recovery. Through the first week of July, steel production for the year was up 27.6 percent from the same period a year earlier. Production through July, 1984, had used 75.8 percent of the industry's capacity, up from 53.2 percent a year earlier.[7] Employment, too, had showed definite signs of recovery. Steel employment in May climbed to 181,174, 7.2 percent above its 1983 low of 168,852. There have been few such propitious moments to draw the line on further trade restrictions.

Finally, the counter strategy had been developed; it lacked only thoughtful articulation. This included implementation of a simpler tax with lower marginal tax rates to further spur increases in production and employment while improving the international competitiveness of the domestic steel industry and the U.S. economy as well as restoration of a monetary standard and the resultant low increase rates to facilitate the industrial revival evidenced in the United States.

The 1979-81 base period chosen for the quotas favors the Japanese and Europeans. But the Latin American countries argued that their ability to service their debt, and in the case of Argentina in particular, to maintain democratic institutions, required added consideration in the form of somewhat higher quotas. Within two days after the ITC announced its recommendation, Argentina was asking for a quota larger than that recommended by the ITC. Korea was expected to make similar appeals. These countries, it seems, were quite willing to cooperate in the cartelization of the U.S. steel market, as long as they received their share of the extra profits created by the trade restrictions.

The danger inherent in such a "don't-rock-the-boat" approach was that it invited similar restrictionist moves by the United States' trading partners. Earlier this year, for example, the European Economic Community responded to the 1983 U.S. decision to restrict specialty steel imports by raising tariffs on selected petrochemicals, sporting goods, and safety devices. Like the current situation, the U.S. trade restrictions were imposed under the injury clause of the 1974 Trade Act. As a result, the EEC's retaliation was within the provisions of the General Agreements on Tariffs and Trade. Thus, it was more than likely that placing limits on foreign steel would be met with added restrictions on U.S. exporters.

Domestic users of steel were strangely quiet in the face of an estimated 10 percent increase in their steel costs. Of the big three automakers, only Chrysler had taken a position on the quotas, and that was to support the steel industry. But then, how can a company that says it is more dependent than ever upon trade restrictions argue against them? Similarly, the machine tool industry, which is suffering from foreign competition, was silent on this government-imposed increase in the price of its steel. It, too, seeks protection from foreign competition.

Evidence of such logrolling is all about. The Simpson-Mazzoli bill's effort to limit the flow of workers—referred to in the pejorative as illegal aliens—into the United States is the worst kind of trade restriction. The notion that a flood of foreign workers will lower the wage rate in the United States rests on a static view of the world. If the capital available to the economy is fixed, then it follows directly that an increase in the supply of labor will lower the wage rate until the demand for labor equals its now greater supply. Even in this worst case scenario, however, output and profits rise, more than offsetting the cumulative effect of any wage fall.

But it is far from clear than an influx of workers means lower wages. Once the supply of capital responds to the new opportunities created by the influx of labor, then the demand for labor will rise right along with its supply. In this case, the returns to capital and labor will remain unchanged, while total output and employment and profits again rise. All are literally made better off. Foreign workers obtain better jobs while Americans have more opportunities to employ their hardearned savings.

This dynamic result appears to be the experience of Southern California. In San Diego an Orange Counties, where the number of illegals is legend, unemployment rates are more than two percentage points below the national and the California average. Property values remain strong, as does regional growth in output and employment.

At some point, the need to stop further impediments to trade must be faced squarely. The alternative is to slide ever so slowly into a protectionist trap which promises only global financial crisis and another recession.

THE STEEL DECISION

President Reagan's response to the U.S. International Trade Commission's recommendation to impose quotas and tariffs on foreign steel was good in word, but bad indeed.

The rhetoric surrounding the decision could not have been better. The ITC's recommendations were "rejected." Such an action, it was argued, would have threatened foreign retaliation, hurting U.S. agriculture and other U.S. exporters. The loss of access to low-cost foreign steel also would threaten jobs in domestic steel fabricating industries. Thus, too many jobs would have been put at risk. This was very much the same logic that had led President Reagan to reject all new restrictions on copper imports.

But in substance, if not in form, the actions promised by Reagan contain the key elements of the ITC's recommendation:[8]

- For the first time, quotas apparently were to be imposed upon virtually all foreign producers. Previously, limits on foreign steel imports had been limited to selected countries.
- The Administration sought to reduce for a give-year period foreign producers' share of the U.S. market. Though the word "target" was eschewed, U.S. Trade Representative William Brock estimated the Administration's efforts would reduce foreign steel to about 20.5 percent of the market from 25.4 percent.
- All steel products were to be covered, including finished products such as sheet and strip, and semifinished products, such as steel slabs. An October 15 deadline was also given Common Market countries to agree "voluntarily" to limit shipments of pipe and tube steel to the United States.

There is validity to the argument that President Reagan made the best out of a bad situation. The steel companies were threatening to file dozens, if not hundreds of lawsuits charging unfair trade practices, and thereby disrupt U.S. trade policy. The industry also was pushing restrictionist legislation in Congress. These efforts were reportedly dropped as a result of the Administration's promise to restrict imports through bilateral negotiations.[9] To argue that the foreign steel producers will "voluntarily" agree to limit their exports to the U.S. market, however, belies the explicit threat contained in the announcement. In cases where a country declines to volunteer, Reagan would be prepared to use the powers granted under the 1974 Trade Act to impose unilaterally import restrictions.[10]

The amount of actual damage done to the economy rests in large measure on the Administration's diligence in negotiating the import restrictions. As past experience has demonstrated, trade patterns rapidly shift to neutralize the effect of restrictions imposed only on selected countries.[11] Thus, the failure to include any country with significant steel capacity would lead to a surge of imports from that country. If the volume were enough to offset the loss of other foreign steel supplies, then world market prices would continue to prevail in the U.S. economy.

Absent such a safety valve, however, steel prices in the United States rise above the world level. Quantity restrictions almost always lead to foreign suppliers concentrating their shipments in their most expensive and highest profit items.[12] Thus, foreign competition would be expected to diminish most noticeably in the lower value-added segments of the steel market.

Moreover, as steel prices rise in the United States domestic fabricators of steel products face a surge of foreign competition. Just as water always seeks the lowest level, so too in an economy that remains as open as the United States to foreign products, consumers will always seek the savings from low-cost foreign steel. Where the products are actually fabricated is of little consequence. The natural result is increased pressure for relief from foreign competition and squeezed profit margins among all steel fabricators.

NOTES AND REFERENCES

1. Eduardo Lachica and Thomas F. Boyle, "ITC Proposes Quotas, Tariffs On Steel Imports," *Wall Street Journal* (July 12, 1984), p. 3.
2. By construction, if the United States does not intervene on the foreign exchange market, then there can be no change in U.S. official reserve assets. In this case, the balance of trade on the current account is equal to but with opposite net foreign capital inflows plus the statistical discrepancy.
3. Victor A. Canto, Richard W. Eastin, and Arthur B. Laffer, "Failure of Protectionism: A Study of the Steel Industry," *Columbia Journal of World Business* XVII (Winter 1982): 43-57.
4. Victor A. Canto and Arthur B. Laffer, "The Incidence of Trade Protection" *Columbia Journal of World Business* XVII (Spring 1982): 60-66.
5. Charles W. Kadlec and Arthur B. Laffer, "Why the Stock Market Declined" (A.B. Laffer Associates, February 22, 1984).
6. Clyde H. Farnsworth, "Panel Asks Protection For Steel," *New York Times* (June 13, 1984).
7. "Steel Output Off in Week," *New York Times* (July 10, 1984), p. 29.
8. Art Pine, "Reagan Vows to Seek Voluntary Steel Import Curbs," *Wall Street Journal* (September 19, 1984), p. 3.
9. Ibid.
10. Ibid.
11. Canto and Laffer, "Failure of Protectionism."
12. Ibid.